Decasualization and Modernization
of Dock Work in London

Students and External Readers

Decasualization and Modernization of Dock Work in London

By Vernon H. Jensen

ILR Paperback No. 9, April 1971

New York State School of Industrial and Labor Relations
A Statutory College of the State University
Cornell University, Ithaca, New York

Price $2.50

ORDER FROM

Publications Division

New York State School of Industrial and Labor Relations

Cornell University, Ithaca 14850

Library of Congress Catalog Card Number: 72–632773

SBN 87546–040–2

PRINTED IN THE UNITED STATES OF AMERICA

BY THE W. F. HUMPHREY PRESS, INC.

Acknowledgments

MY gratitude for the support which the New York State School of Industrial and Labor Relations, Cornell University, extended to me must be expressed first. The School made possible two trips to England which were essential to the prosecution of the study. One of these trips was supported, in part, by the Center for International Studies of Cornell University. For this assistance, I am also grateful.

I enjoyed very fine cooperation from a number of important and strategically situated persons, without whose help neither the necessary information could have been obtained nor many of the nuances in the situation of the docks industry in London understood. The limitations in presentation are mine, as is the responsibility for interpreting and assessing the complicated and many-faceted phenomena laid out in the story detailed in the manuscript. It is impossible to thank everyone, perhaps none adequately, but a number of persons may be named without further effort to describe or weigh their assistance. But many not named, particularly among rank-and-file dockers and persons in the governmental agencies, organizations, and companies visited, are not being overlooked. I thank them.

Without any effort to be partial, let me extend my thanks to Mr. M. R. Haddock, general manager, National Dock Labour Board; his assistant general manager, Mr. J. H. C. Pape, and the manager of the London Office of the board, Mr. W. F. G. Denton, and to those on their staffs who also gave me time or favor; to Mr. Jack L. Jones, general secretary, Transport and General Workers Union; Mr. Timothy O'Leary, national secretary, Docks Group, Transport and General Workers Union, and Mr. Peter Shea, secretary, Docks Group, London, Transport and General Workers Union; to Mr. G. E. Tonge, chairman, National Association of Port Employers and Mr. Eric Bainbridge, general manager, National Association of Port Employers; to Mr. J. K. Badcock, general manager and secretary, London Port Employers' Association; to Mr. D. L. Bennett, general manager, London Ocean Trades' Employer Association; to Mr. G. Dudley Perkins, director general, Port of London Authority, and in particular, to Mr. Stanley Turner, Port of London Authority and Mr. A. Cameron, editor, the *PLA Monthly* who made arrangements for me to receive copies of *The Port;* to Mr. Lionel E. Wigglesworth, Scruttons Maltby, Inc. and several of his associates, Mr. R. H. Hampson, Commander D. J. B. Jewitt, Mr. A. E Jeffrey, and Mr. W. R. Brooks; to Mr. G. B. H. Cattel, Department of Employment and Productivity; and, with special thanks for personal considerations also, to Mr. T. E. Cook, manager, European Marine Operations, United States Lines, and his staff.

V. H. J.

Ithaca, New York
February 3, 1971

Contents

Introduction

HISTORICALLY, in spite of unconscionable conditions and glaring evils, the belief prevailed that the docks industry was a victim of circumstances beyond its control; that regrettable as these conditions were acknowledged to be (although many employers did not seem to regret them) nothing could be done to eliminate, even to ease, the hardships of casual work. Consequently, if the casual labor market was not openly defended, until recently little was done within the industry to improve it, let alone to eliminate this type of labor market.

Although, under various types of pressure, attempts to restructure the labor market or to offer protection against its harshness have been made in many of the ports of the world in recent years, in most of them the casual labor market, cankerous as it is, is still believed to be an inevitable product of shipping. Even where beliefs have changed, the conditions and attitudes produced by casual dock work live on to plague the industry, now especially noticeable when revolutionary changes in methods of cargo handling cry for rapid acceptance. In fact, the introduction of such changes and the accompanying mechanization are seriously impeded by the attitudes of casualness still prevailing among both men and employers.

Until recently, too, employers in the docks industry appeared to be unaware of, or kept their eyes closed to, the hidden costs of casual labor. Indeed, many employers liked the arrangements because of the profits they could make within them; around the world, many still seem to like them. The truth is, of course, that employers have not been paying the full cost of their labor, with the result that they have not been forced to consider the economies of different employment conditions; or, put differently, the diseconomies of casual labor have not been added up. The convenience of having a ready supply of workers at beck and call brought about costs that could have been avoided, many of which the employers would not have accepted had they had to pay them. Among the men, the conditions of casualness produced defensive and self-serving reactions and attitudes which created fixed customs and practices. Yet, like the employers, many liked the arrangement — enjoying the lack of discipline associated with a casual labor market and keeping their eyes closed to the terrific costs it imposed upon them. Nevertheless, the glaring fact, both from the social and general economic point of view, is that social and economic costs to the community have been appalling and largely unnecessary.

While it has taken some a long time to reach such conclusions, others have cried out repeatedly against the unconscionable continuation of evils and suffering associated with casual labor, and the unwitting or careless imposition of its cost upon society, until, as noted, changes have been taking place in various ports and countries. Of real significance are those being achieved in England, where the tenacity of casualness has persisted for years, even in the face of a long series of notable reports by prominent critics of its evils.[1] For instance, the National

---

[1] For several early reports, see: S. and B. Webb (eds.) *The Public Organization of the Labour Market: Being Part Two of the Ministry Report of the Poor Law Commission* (London: Longmans, Green and Co., 1909); W. Beveridge, *Unemployment: A Problem of Industry* (London: Longmans, Green and Co., 1912), pp. 81–95; Transport Workers, Court of Inquiry, *Report and Minutes of Evidence of the Inquiry*, 2 vols. (1920) Cmnd. 936 and 937; E. C. P. Lascelles and S. S. Bullock, *Dock Labour and Decasualization* (London: P. S. King and Son, 1924). For most notable of

Dock Labour Scheme, instituted during World War II through the efforts of Ernest Bevin and established legislation afterward, and hailed as a great step forward, as it was, did little more than force certain ameliorations of the conditions which casualness produced — certain defenses against the evils it spawned. Mistakenly, many persons thought that the Scheme, presided over by the National Dock Labour Board (NDLB), had corrected the basic evils of dock employment in England. This, unhappily, was not so. But a series of developments since has led step by step to complete decasualization of the labor force. Every dock worker is now in permanent engagement with an employer. In part, the employers also have been decasualized, a necessary preliminary to decasualization of the men. The system is to an extent self-decasualizing, for the costs of maintaining the labor force must be borne continuously by those who use it. Those who cannot carry the costs have largely left, or will leave, the industry.

Friday, September 15, 1967, marked the end of the casual system; Monday, the 18th, the beginning of a new era. The event is significant indeed, but casualness dies hard. At best, there were found to be many difficulties in introducing such a revolutionary program; "teething" problems of various sorts were fully expected. One does not wave away narrow, private, and institutionalized interests as with a wand. Many arrangements and specific interim protections had to be agreed to. Consensus was obviously impossible; all the existing or potential problems in the complexities of this unusually complex

more recent governmental reports, see: Ministry of Labour and National Service, *Port Transport Industry Report* (London: His Majesty's Stationery Office, 1946); Ministry of Labour and National Service, *Unofficial Stoppages in the London Docks,* Report of Committee of Inquiry (Leggett Committee) (London: His Majesty's Stationery Office, 1951); Ministry of Labour and National Service, *Port Transport Industry, Report of a Committee appointed to inquire into the operation of the dock workers (Regulation of Employment) Scheme, 1947* (Devlin Report) (London: Her Majesty's Stationery Office, 1956); Ministry of Transport, *Report of the Committee of Inquiry into Major Ports of Great Britain* (London: Her Majesty's Printing Office, Cmnd. 1824, 1962).

industry could not be anticipated. And, even when almost everyone who was seriously concerned was hailing the new day, opponents and disruptors were creating unnecessary obstacles; some radicals, ironically, did not want decasualization; deliberate obfuscation and opposition were added to the difficulties.

Although it is too early to evaluate all the changes and benefits of the experience, a report of the development of the program, of what had to be done to bring it off, how it was accomplished, and the experience under it is possible and worth the telling. Events following decasualization, some of them appalling to many, can be reviewed and analyzed. To the social scientist, this better ordering of a labor market and more efficient use of resources is interesting, both as a case study and as an experiment in rule-making of a far-reaching kind in a complex setting, including some important ideological differences. To the men, the unions, the employers, the Government, and to the economic and social communities of England it is a program of widespread economic and social reform carrying great promise. Its achievement has been laborious, often heartbreaking, and not simply because of the accompanying and interrelated issue of nationalization of the industry.

Background and Developments

Literature on the need and desirability of decasualization of dock work in England is extensive. Earlier efforts to do something about the problem have a long history, which I have covered elsewhere.[2] Only the recent story is told here. Mostly, it deals with London, although the national view is sometimes in focus.

It has long been recognized but, as noted, not generally understood, that the National Dock Labour Scheme did not produce decasualization. Actually, its framers never intended that it should, nor, under the economic and institutional con-

[2]V. H. Jensen, *Hiring of Dock Workers and Employment Practices in the Ports of New York, Liverpool, London, Rotterdam, and Marseilles* (Cambridge, Mass.: Harvard University Press, 1964), pp. 121–214.

ditions of the time, is it likely they could have done much more than they did. Not that decasualization could not have come sooner, but there is an explanation why it did not.

In March 1961, the Minister of Transport, Ernest Marples, appointed a Committee of Inquiry to consider the extent to which the docks and harbors of Great Britain were adequate to meet national needs and how the methods of working in them could be improved. Known as the Rochdale Committee, by virtue of its chairman, Lord Rochdale, it carried out its broad investigation and reported in July 1962.[3] One of the eight substantive sections of the report deals with dock labor. Four chapters in that section cover the background of the unions and negotiating machinery, the National Dock Labour Scheme, decasualization, and various other aspects of dock labor.

While its investigations were being conducted (partly because of them, perhaps, but also because of other pressures at work), the National Joint Council for the Port Transport Industry (NJC), the national negotiating body for the industry, published its conclusion on June 6, 1961 that decasualization was the basic solution to problems of the docks industry. A Working Party to look into the problems was established. An agreement was reached, and a policy directive to all the local joint committees in the industry was issued in October 1961.[4] This is an historic document, commonly referred to as the "Crichton-Cousins Accord," in which management and labor forthrightly stated jointly that "the background to industrial relations in the docks, and the source of most of the industry's special problems, [had] been the casual system of employment." Recognition was given to the fact that the National Dock Labour Scheme, "with its control of the registers, and its attendance money and guarantee benefits in case of underemployment," had only tried to offset effects of the casual system of engagement. Allowing that "average earnings" in the docks were

[3]Ministry of Transport, *op. cit.*

[4]The National Joint Council for the Port Transport Industry, "Policy Directive to All Local Joint Committees on Decasualization," October 1961, mimeo.; cf. Ministry of Transport, *op. cit.*, Appendix N, pp. 262–264.

"regularly among the highest in industry," as well as noting the "recently instituted Pension and Training Schemes," it candidly said, nevertheless, that:

(i) The basis of engagement and employment for the majority of men is still casual. The Dock Labour Scheme benefits and high average earnings do not prevent wide fluctuations in the individual's earnings from week to week, and wide fluctuations in earnings between individuals, from this has followed:

(ii) The casual attitude towards the observance of agreements and conciliation procedures, as exemplified by the industry's experience of strikes.

(iii) The casual attitude militating against the efficient use of manpower, as exemplified by resistance to modern methods including mechanization and by adherence to restrictive practices.

Acknowledging that the casual attitude and the practices following from it militated against the true interests of dock workers and employers alike, the Accord continued, "the time [had] come for a fresh and bold advance towards effective decasualization with the object of decasualizing both employment and relationships in the industry." It was cautious in recognizing obstacles — which the cynic might interpret as prior excuse for probable failure — clearly "the greatest regard must be paid, as in all dock affairs, to the variations in the situation from port to port." Fluctuations in requirements for labor "present the greatest obstacle to solving the problems of decasualization." Some, related to fluctuations in the volume of cargo, "are beyond the control of either Port Employers or Dockworkers" and "in some cases, are so extreme and irregular as to make effective decasualization impracticable at this stage." Over-all, "the real obstacle to more effective decasualization [had] been a lack of flexibility in the deployment of labour in the most effective manner possible." That inflexibility could be eliminated by cooperation of the employers and dock workers, the directive recognized, but noted that effective deployment of the labor force was inhibited by one, or a combination of, rigid manning scales, multiplicity of employers some of whom engaged labor very intermittently, and restrictions on the use of mechanical aids. To overcome all of these obstacles would "require a profound change of thought and approach by all concerned in the industry. But they [had to] be overcome if dockworkers [were] to achieve real regularity of employment and earnings and if the industry [were] to give the service the community [was] entitled to expect." In retrospect, it is clear that the top echelons on each side of the industry recognized the dimensions of the problems.

The NJC immediately called upon the local joint committees in the respective ports to study and report by January 1, 1962 on the practicability, in relation to their port circumstances, of a substantial advance toward effective decasualization on the basis of the following principles:

(i) Preservation of the Dock Labour Scheme.

(ii) Engagement of the substantial majority of the men on the register on a weekly basis, either by individual employers or by groups of employers, or by employers generally.

(iii) Without compulsion upon any dockworker to enter into a weekly engagement or upon an individual employer to engage a particular dockworker on weekly terms the expectation on the part of every entrant to the industry that he will after an appropriate period of satisfactory service be considered for a weekly engagement. Due regard to be paid to maintaining the balance in specialist grades.

(iv) Possible allocation in rotation to employment of men not covered by weekly engagement.

(v) Abolition of restrictive practices including all practices inhibiting the mobility of labour.

(vi) Fullest possible economic use of mechanical aids.

(vii) Adoption of shift systems where appropriate, either as a general basis of operation or as the best means of deploying the labour force.[5]

The Rochdale Committee, in its conclusions and recommendations on decasualization, supported and reinforced the conclusions and program of the NJC, recognizing also that

[5]*Ibid.*

decasualization would have to be accompanied by a reduction in the number of employers, increased flexibility in deployment of men, and by greater use of mechanical aids. It recognized that the financial aspects needed careful study, but felt that action was so urgent that the parties should "press ahead with arrangements for the greatest possible degree of decasualization of dock labour, within the Dock Labour Scheme" and urged that port authorities be given statutory powers to formulate conditions of licensing employers with the view of reducing "the number of employers to a reasonable level."[6] It was also concerned with training. As to the provision of decent amenities on the docks, notwithstanding the fact that everyone had long known of this dire need, it could only recommend study.

It is curious that, although the elements of decasualization were all recognized and the framework of the approach laid out under which decasualization would come, it would take five years to bring it off as Stage I in a two-stage plan. Even then, some major and some ancillary problems would slide into Stage II — planned modernization — the *quid pro quo* for the first. The events and developments under modernization, following decasualization, comprise the second half of the total story.

In the five years up to September 1967, the problems and concepts of the decasualization scheme got a good mulling over — some might say, mauling. Perhaps certain requirements of the rule-making process had to run their course. People had to be prepared, and the complexities and involved interrelationship of issues sorted out. The issues had to be debated among the various groups having interests at stake and the power factors assessed. The chief spokesmen and leaders for each side of the industry were aware that consent within the affected constituent groups was imperative. In all fairness and honesty, the pecuniary interests of various groups on each side had to be considered and arrangements made to meet them. Dock workers had to be convinced that they would

---

[6]Ministry of Transport, *op. cit.*, pp. 144–145.

gain more than they were giving up. Many employers had to be assured that the costs of the changes would be recoverable within a reasonable time. Not least, the Government, and the politics of it, were always involved directly or indirectly. Ideological differences extant in the industry bedeviled all the parties.

Without doubt, the major obstacle delaying effectuation of decasualization in 1963 was the failure of local negotiations and the inability, through them, to match at that level the consensus on general principles which had been reached at the national level. The fact is that while agreement had been reached at the national level on the general approach there was not complete agreement, even at that level, on the import and application of all seven principles in the Crichton-Cousins Accord. However, even if there had been full agreement at the national level on the import and application of the general principles, this would not have led automatically to consensus on them at the local level. Much more than inadequate communication, the real problem was in finding workable and acceptable operating arrangements necessitating the accommodation of a variety of deep-seated economic interests — some of them ideological and, perhaps, not subject to compromise.

The charge to the local negotiating bodies quickly led to queries from them on both sides throughout the industry. These matters came back to the national level for further consideration and instructions. The NJC could not, however, agree on a more explicit directive to the local bodies.

Each side thereafter prepared its own observations and sent them to its constituents at the local level. By early 1963, their basic differences were revealed. The employers conceded the necessity of preserving the National Dock Labour Scheme — apparently a *sine qua non* of the unions and the men — and were willing to say that decasualization would not result in redundancy or discharge of men from the industry, either initially or as a result of increased efficiency; any necessary reduction in the labor force would be effectuated by natural wastage and control of recruitment. But with regard to the

matter of permanent engagement, the employers were not willing to shoulder substantial extra cost at the outset of decasualization without definite arrangements for more efficient use
and deployment of men. They wanted to know in advance
what they would get for payment of a weekly guaranteed wage.

On its part, the union side had already made it clear in
response to the recommendations of the Rochdale Report, that
decasualization could have no exceptions: the opportunity for
regular employment had to be made available to all men, not
just to an enlarged group of weekly workers. The unionists
reaffirmed this and their earlier insistence on having the NDLB
as the agency for application of any agreements to decasualize.
They again made it clear they would accept no redundancy.
At this stage they were willing only to state the premise that,
as a result of decasualization and improved methods, there
would be "greater efficiency," but qualified it with "better
earnings." They were not willing to say that improvements
could or would be a prior condition of decasualization. The
view of the unions was that improvements in efficiency could be
no more than a result to be expected — that is, decasualization
had to come first — the matter of efficiency from changed working practices would follow.

This difference between the parties became a major obstacle
particularly to agreement on the size of the basic guarantee —
the unions' view being that, until the amount of the basic
guarantee was known, they could not agree to changed working conditions; the employers', that they could not go beyond
an offer of £ 11 until they knew in advance what concessions
they would receive on working arrangements.[7]

London — Employer Associations and Unions

Since the Port of London from here on provides our primary
focus, its complex of unions and groups of employers should

[7]Ministry of Labour, *Final Report of the Committee of Inquiry under
the Rt. Hon. Lord Devlin into Certain Matters Concerning the Port Transport Industry* (London: Her Majesty's Stationery Office, Cmnd. 2734, August
1965), pp. 58–59. This contains a detailed report of the various local negotiations in several of the major local ports (see pp. 50–87).

be briefly explained and related to the national bodies. The NJC, the national bargaining body, has been identified already. It is composed of representatives from the National Association of Port Employers (NAPE) and the Dockers Section of the Transport and General Workers Union. The national headquarters of each are in London and what happens in London is of importance nationally. But national developments also are of concern in London. It may be noted that for a number of years the National Association of Stevedores and Dock Workers (NASD) has not had representatives on the NJC.

The local joint body in London is the Port of London Local Joint Committee, composed of representatives of the Port Employers of London and of the TGWU and the NASD. But there are other local joint groups which exist under the over-all "umbrella" of the Port of London Local Joint Committee, whose representatives come from counterpart management and labor organizations. The chart below shows the general structure at the outset of the negotiations in the early 1960's.

The short-sea trades, the coast-wide shipping, has virtually faded out and the two wharfinger employer groups have combined into one. The concern of this body is to the Riverside, as distinguished from the Enclosed Docks. Lighterage is concerned with movement of barges on the river, and is a diminishing activity. To be noted particularly is the recent formation of a new consolidated employer association, London Ocean Trades Employer Association (LOTEA). The LSDLC was left as the employer policy-making body, while the LOTEA has become the negotiating body, except for the PLA, but coordinated bargaining is the practice.

The Dockers Section of the TGWU in London is comprised of several branches; too many, most people think. The branches are grouped by sections: for example, the Enclosed Docks, Riverside, Lighterage, and OST Clerks. Representatives from the sections, two from each of six, plus one from the outports, comprise the No. 1 Docks Group Committee.[8] A representative from the TGWU staff serves as secretary. This committee is a

---

[8]*The Port,* March 13, 1969, pp. 8–9.

The Labor and Management Structure in the Port of London

Employers' Groups	Unions

Employers' Groups		Unions
Port Employers of London	Port of London Local Joint Committee	
	Port Labour Executive Committee	TGWU NASD
London Shipowners Dock Labour Committee (LSDLC)	Ocean Shipowners Group Committee	TGWU NASD
London Short-Sea Traders Association	Short-Sea Traders Joint Board	TGWU
Port of London Authority (PLA)	Port of London Group Labour Committee	TGWU
London Association of Public Wharfingers	Wharfingers Group Joint Committee A	TGWU
Federation of Public Wharfingers	Wharfingers Group Joint Committee B	TGWU NASD (Dockers)
Association of Master Lightermen and Barge Owners	London Lighterage Joint Committee	WLTBU TGWU (Waterways)

policy-making body, not a negotiating body, but, as will be seen, is very powerful.

Although not important for our purposes, mention should also be made of the fact that within the TGWU are so-called lay committees; for example, the Ocean Lay Committee, the Wharfinger Lay Committee, the PLA Lay Committee, and the OST Clerks Lay Committee. They are responsible for over-all administration of agreements and the day-to-day problems arising under them.

The NASD, commonly referred to as the "Blue Union," is a power to contend with. It has a jurisdiction which overlaps functionally and geographically with that of the TGWU. It sometimes cooperates, but sometimes does not, and has a longstanding rule that policy and decisions must be made in open meetings of the members.

In spite of claims by some employers in London that they could have achieved decasualization much earlier and without governmental intervention, local negotiations in London in 1963 and 1964 did not achieve agreement. As it turned out, there were four sets of local negotiations: the Enclosed Docks, the Wharfingers or Riverside, Lighterage, and OST Clerks. Along the way, when the viewpoint emerged that there was no need for separate agreements, the wharfinger negotiations were merged with those of the enclosed docks. The unions generally took the view that there should be only one plan for the whole port, but employers had diverse interests. While progress was made in all negotiations, but particularly in those of the light-erage group and tally clerks, great difficulties were experienced in the Enclosed Docks Committee, where, in early 1963, the terms of employment became the stickiest issue.

Both the PLA and other employers submitted comprehensive lists of improved working conditions proposed by them, which the union said it would examine. But the proposals were laid before a mass meeting of the Blue Union, and the unofficial, self-styled Port Workers Liaison Committee (hereafter referred to as the unofficial Liaison Committee) — a body generally considered to be Communist-dominated, if not led, and comprised of dock workers from the several unions, but principally from the TGWU — also got access to them. At the Blue Union meeting, the employers' proposals were condemned vigorously. Afterward, the unofficial Liaison Committee started a campaign against them. Since the issues raised touched the men closely, it was not difficult to arouse them emotionally. The employers were greatly disturbed because they had thought the documents would be held in confidence as negotiating instruments only.

Almost everywhere, not alone in London, insurmountable difficulties beset the parties. They were not bargaining to a dead-line, and the matter was too big and complicated to be forced by economic action; that is, by taking a strike or by striking. The trade union side was not sufficiently unified on a program to follow such a route, in any event. The complexities in London made communications even more difficult than normally. The failure of communication in the unions, particularly in the TGWU, have been commented upon frequently. One of the leaders of the Blue Union, which had a tradition of rank-and-file activity, in explaining the rejection of the employers' proposals, put the matter realistically: "We were given too much to handle at one time...it was too much... to place in one document." He felt that if it had come in pieces over a period of time they might have carried on better.[9]

Hours of Work, Overtime, and Wages

Because immediate questions of hours of work and overtime had been hanging fire for some time and a new national wage demand arose, the parties diverted their attention to them, and the effort to achieve a program of decasualization was simply set aside. Nevertheless, as will be seen, the dispute over wages in 1964 led to the creation of a new forum, the Devlin Committee, for consideration of decasualization.

An agreement to establish a 40-hour work week had been negotiated in October 1963 and was set to be implemented in July 1964, but the Blue Union put a ban against weekend working. The unofficial Liaison Committee did likewise. The dispute about overtime merged with the wages claim. No doubt the wages claim took the employers by surprise. An agreement by the joint committee was rejected by a National Delegate Conference of the TGWU. This led directly to the appointment of the Devlin Committee to consider, first, the wages issue, afterward, the whole subject of decasualization.

---

[9]Ministry of Labour, *op. cit.*, pp. 56–57.

Devlin Committee

BECAUSE of prior unofficial strikes, continuing difficulties over work-week issues, and the threat of a work stoppage over wages, it had been decided by the Government that prompt resolution of the wages dispute was desirable. Although it was recognized that prospect of decasualization carried serious implications for the whole wage structure of the industry, and that this had led employers to be cautious about the amount of any increase they might offer, an interim payment of some amount could be recommended. The Devlin Committee then would turn its attention to an appraisal of the structure and practices of the industry, including all aspects of wages and conditions of employment. The dispute over wages was settled for the time being.[10]

The Devlin Committee then pursued its assignment on decasualization, but the parties were not prepared to make their presentations until January 1965. In private meetings supplemented with investigations by members of the Committee, the

---

[10]Ministry of Labour, *First Report of the Committee of Inquiry into Certain Matters Concerning the Port Transport Industry* (London: Her Majesty's Stationery Office, Cmnd. 2523, November 1964), pp. 3–15.

facts were assembled. A very complete and full review and analysis of the industry was made in the report issued on August 5, 1965.

The Devlin Committee found dissension and inefficiency in the industry and the same conditions that had often been revealed before: dockers' lack of security, preferential treatment of "blue-eyed boys," dockers' lack of responsibility, defects in management, time-wasting practices, piecework complexities and inadequacies, restrictions on overtime and shift working, woefully inadequate welfare amenities, and trade union organizational difficulties. Casual management as well as casual labor came in for specific criticism. "We are satisfied," the Committee said, "that the casual employer is a cause of both inefficiency and dissension." It was stated that the casual employer had to go, that "casual employment makes it difficult for employers generally...to develop competent personnel policies." In turn, the unions were criticized for lack of control and for the "absence of a shop steward system." Time-wasting practices, whether protective or restrictive, which prolonged the jobs were criticized, particularly the working of the "continuity rule."[11] Bad timekeeping, excessive manning, and "welting" and "spelling," under which only part of the men were at work at a given time, were likewise criticized.

Of great interest is the discussion of union difficulties. Multiple unions, the two main ones with partially overlapping jurisdictions and diverse views about union activities and operations, as well as the unofficial Liaison Committee, added up to trouble. The unofficial Liaison Committee was seen as more concerned "to disrupt the working of the port as often and as seriously as possible" than "to improve dock workers' conditions" and was found to be against decasualization because "anything that makes for good industrial relations is bad for wrecking," held to be the primary aim of this group. In turn,

---

[11]Ministry of Labour, *Final Report of the Committee of Inquiry under the Rt. Hon. Lord Devlin into Certain Matters Concerning the Port Transport Industry*, pp. 12–16; for an explanation and discussion of the "continuity rule," see V. H. Jensen, *op. cit.*, pp. 203 ff.

the TGWU was severely criticized for allowing the unofficial leadership to become a rival power.[12]

The Devlin Committee listed nine things that would have to be done before peace and efficiency could be achieved on the docks:

(1) Elimination of the casual employer and of casual management;

(2) Introduction of a system of regular employment;

(3) Establishing strong and effective trade union leadership;

(4) Obtaining of greater mobility of labour;

(5) Improvement of welfare facilities;

(6) Revision of the wage structure;

(7) Abolition of time-wasting practices;

(8) Acceptance of firmer discipline, particularly in the matter of timekeeping and in respect for decisions of the Board;

(9) Review of manning scales to take into account increasing mechanization and changing methods.[13]

What was needed, it was said, was modernization of labor relations and new techniques of leadership and persuasion to secure normal and regular employment under the National Dock Labour Scheme as well as work sharing and equality of treatment without redundancy. The Devlin Committee recognized an industrial relations stalemate on the docks because negotiations on decasualization had petered out. It looked at "buying the book," that is, the approach on the United States west coast — where the employers, by the establishment of a sizable fund to provide for a variety of benefits to the workers, obtained the freedom to eliminate restrictive practices and to modernize; and at the more conventional approach on the east coast of the U. S. — where the employers and the union joined a guarantee of annual employment with reduction in size of gangs and elimination of certain restrictive practices; it looked at the possible nationalization of the port transport industry, and at the question of whether the labor force could be administered by the National Dock Labour Board under

[12]Ministry of Labour, *Final Report...*, pp. 2–46.

[13]*Ibid.*, p. 88.

the Scheme as an operational employer or as a holding employer in conjunction with individual employers, possibly as in Rotterdam.[14]

The Committee rejected all these alternative remedies. "One of the reasons for the failure of negotiations hitherto seems to us to be that the parties were trying to do too much," the Committee believed. "It might be that the employers were trying to buy too much for too little. But even if they had been willing to pay more, we doubt if the trade union leaders could have obtained from their followers a real and comprehending assent to long lists of improved working arrangements....What is wanted is a real assent and understanding from the bulk of the men and for that purpose the deal must be made much simpler. The basic things must be tackled first."[15] Accordingly, the first three items in its list, elimination of the casual employer, introduction of regular employment, and strong union leadership, were declared basic but intertwined. Also basic was the fourth, greater mobility of labor, but thought best achieved in two stages. It was said, "a new plan for regular employment must shed at once practices that are clearly identifiable with the casual era," but other restrictive practices could wait for subsequent negotiations. The improvement of welfare facilities could go ahead independently. The remaining items could be subordinated "to the conclusion of the basic settlement" or handled in a subsequent phase.

It recommended that employers "prepare schemes for the reduction of employers and for action by those who remain," that the TGWU "restore and strengthen its authority," that the NDLB "prepare a scheme for improvement of welfare facilites," that the NJC "resume negotiations on a plan for regular employment" inclusive of representation of the NASD, and that the Government arm itself "with such powers as are nec-

[14]*Ibid.*, pp. 90 ff.; cf. International Longshoremen's and Warehousemen's Union and Pacific Maritime Association, *Men and Machines*—a story of the mechanization and modernization agreement, 1963; V. H. Jensen, "Computer Hiring of Dock Workers in the Port of New York," *Industrial and Labor Relations Review*, April 1967, pp. 414 ff.

[15]Ministry of Labour, *Final Report...*, p. 102.

essary to drive through, if need be, the reorganization of the industry."[16]

With the conclusion that "the best line of approach to the reform of industrial relations on the docks" was the national policy directive of October 1961, the Devlin Committee laid out a detailed plan of action, noting that the failure to achieve modernization in prior negotiations was based on two factors:

(1) Too little was allowed in the way of decasualization and too much in the way of abolition of restrictive practices;

(2) Neither side had put itself in a position to negotiate and carry out the sort of reform that was needed, the employers' side because they were still burdened with the dead weight of casual employment and the trade union side because they had not as a body done enough to prepare their membership for the reception of new ideas.[17]

The plan of action directed the NJC to issue a new directive, remedying the deficiencies of the old one. With respect to each of the seven principles enumerated in the Crichton-Cousins Accord (see pp. 5–7 above), the Devlin Committee gave detailed recommendations. Taking them seriatim, first, preservation of the National Dock Labour Scheme, meant preservation of the spirit of the Scheme and the fundamental guarantees, including joint control over the size of the register. Also administration of discipline had to be extended to cover permanent men, with the Board alone having power to dismiss them. On the second, third, and fourth principles in the old directive, which called for engagement of a substantial majority of the men on a weekly basis, without compulsion upon any dock worker to enter into weekly engagement or upon an individual employer to engage a particular worker, and the possibility of allocation in rotation to employment of men not covered by weekly engagement, it was said, "these principles must now be reshaped and restated so as to provide for regular employment." The objective was to be full decasualization; that is, engagement on a weekly basis of all men on the register, but

[16]*Ibid.*, pp. 102 ff.
[17]*Ibid.*, p. 125.

with arrangements for limited temporary transfers among employers to meet fluctuations in demand.

Regarding the fifth principle, the abolition of restrictive practices, including all practices inhibiting the mobility of labor, a distinction had to be drawn between those restrictions which were essentially a feature of the casual method of employment, classed in a category A, and all other restrictions, classed in a category B. However logical, this division led to later difficulties. The sixth principle, the fullest possible economic use of mechanical aids, was to be considered in conjunction with review of the wage structure, particularly review of piecework and overtime payments in relation to basic rates of pay. The seventh principle, adoption of shift systems where appropriate, was to be tackled after the new system of employment was in effect and working properly.

The subjects in principles number one through four and the restrictive practices in category A were to be matters of immediate negotiations — the first part of a new settlement which came to be referred to as Devlin Stage I. The restrictive practices in category B and the fullest possible economic use of mechanical aids were to be negotiated together as a second part of a new settlement (Devlin Stage II). Benefits of increased productivity, it was understood, were to be shared, and unresolved differences were to be dealt with by the negotiating committee under a prescribed procedure.

Following the new directive, each side of the industry was admonished to prepare to negotiate immediately. For employers, this meant reduction in their number and preparation by each of those remaining to employ his quota of men and provide for their welfare and supervision. For the TGWU, it meant a campaign for restoration of authority and influence in the ports of London, Liverpool, and Hull, and for explanation of the new directive to the men. For the NASD, it meant granting authority to its leaders to negotiate in conformity with the new directive.

The NDLB was directed to make a comprehensive survey of the need for facilities and amenities for dock workers in each port, especially of amenities to be provided by individual employers under the Board's supervision and of those which could be provided only in cooperation with other public authorities.

The Government was to be prepared to impose a scheme on the industry if the NJC could not agree on a new directive or if it refused to form a negotiating committee seating the Blue Union as well as an independent element; if the independent element were to report that negotiations were not making suitable progress; or if it became necessary to act to ensure that an agreed plan was not wrecked by a minority.[18]

Implementing the Devlin Recommendations

Both employers and unions quickly accepted the report and recommendations. With all the publicity given and with the Government determined to see action, the employers had little choice, but their acceptance was genuine and they set out promptly to start things moving. As will easily be shown, their task, not to mention the Government's, was complex and many-faceted.

Was this to be another effort without results, asked the skeptics? Remarks by the *Economist* revealed a mixture of enthusiasm and skepticism. Critical of the first, or interim, Devlin Report because it "perpetrated all the usual (and manifold) inflationary errors that arbitrators are apt to perpetrate" — it had recommended an increase in wages – the *Economist* praised the major Devlin Report. Yet of the first report it conceded that "maybe its error bought it good will;" in retrospect, it did mollify the workers. But it was the major report that the *Economist* ecstatically saw as putting the Devlin Committee "on the side of the angels," and yet solemnly viewed it as a test of Great Britain's ability to change and as a challenge to the Government to prove that it could produce fundamental change.

While praising "clear recommendations," the *Economist* observed that "the responsible bodies" would doubtless be "un-

---

[18]*Ibid.*, pp. 125–129.

willing or unable to swallow the nasty but necessary medicine" offered and, consequently, enjoined the Government to ready plans for action. Quite accurately, it saw the new proposals as an implementation of the Crichton-Cousins Accord which, in spite of the blessing it had received from the leaders of both sides, had "sunk into a morass of committees and memoranda and inaction." This was not to be repeated. For its part, the *Economist* had difficulty seeing the need, if there was to be a permanent rather than casual relationship, of retaining the National Dock Labour Scheme which, it said, "interposes a syndicalist body between employers and employees." (It did not appreciate the deep feelings of the men on the necessity of keeping the NDLB.) It quite correctly held that "neither party to the negotiations that are necessary, if decasualization is to be pushed through, is competent to do the pushing." Government help would be necessary. Hence, with some un-kindliness, it urged that they "be pushed until they become competent." Decasualization of employers was looked upon as "mercy killing," while the unions were seen as incompetent as proven by the "incidence of unofficial strikes" and the "success of a few piffling agitators."[19]

New Policy Directive

Four days after the Devlin Report was issued, the Minister of Labour, Mr. Ray Gunter, held meetings with representatives of the NAPE and the trade unions. He emphasized the importance which the Government attached to speedy implementation of the recommendations. Thereafter, the NJC met several times. Before a month had passed, it had agreed upon a new policy directive for modernization of industrial relations on the docks:

(1) Preservation of the principles of the Dock Labour Scheme;

(2) Regular employment on a weekly basis by individual employers of all dockworkers;

(3) Development of an adequate sick pay scheme and review of the pension arrangements;

[19]*The Economist,* August 7, 1965, pp. 504–505.

(4) Acceptance of the principle of the transferability of men on a temporary basis between employers;

(5) Acceptance of the principle of work sharing;

(6) Abolition of all restrictive practices essentially a feature of the casual method of employment;

(7) Pledging that the modernization agreement would not lead to the discharge of men from the industry;

(8) Licensing of port employers by the National Ports Council.

In addition the NJC, agreeing on the two-stage phasing laid down by the Devlin Committee, established a national modernization committee, determined its functions, and agreed upon the procedure for setting up local modernization committees.[20]

National Modernization Committee

The National Modernization Committee (NMC) was made up of four members appointed by the Minister of Labour: Lord Brown, chairman, Glacier Metal Company; Mr. Z. T. Claro, chief conciliation officer of the Ministry of Labour; Sir William G. Garrett, former president, British Employers Confederation; Mr. G. H. Doughty, general secretary, Draughtsmen and Allied Technicians Association; and seven employer and seven union members, who for the most part, came from the NJC, naturally interlocking the two bodies. The NJC retained its functions of negotiating on industrial matters, as it always did, while the NMC concerned itself solely with the assignments given to it under modernization.

Representation of the NASD presented a problem. In spite of certain long-standing differences with the TGWU, as noted above, the NASD once held membership on the NJC. While both sides of the NJC agreed that the NASD should have representation on the NMC, the Blue Union would have to accept the principles of the National Policy Directive. The NJC, therefore, took steps to obtain assurances, which were eventually provided in a letter signed by the general secretary

[20]National Joint Council for the Port Transport Industry, "National Policy Directive on Modernization of the Docks Industry Based on the Conclusions of the Devlin Committee of Inquiry," Sept. 2, 1965, mimeo.

of the NASD, R. Barrett. This came about as a result of conferences between J. L. Jones and T. O'Leary of the TGWU
and Barrett, in which a new *modus vivendi* between the two
unions was worked out. Confusion followed, however, when
members of the Blue Union in Liverpool, Hull, and Manchester balked. Nevertheless, when Barrett gave reassurances
and repudiated the actions of the dissenters, he was included
among the seven union representatives on the NMC. Shortly,
however, Barrett died suddenly and was replaced by the acting
secretary of the NASD, W. P. Hegarty. It is to be noted, also,
that the Lightermen in London also had a representative.

The NMC went to work in earnest and held ten meetings
before the end of the year, taking up the main subjects of
wages structure, sick pay scheme, improvements in pension benefits, and abolition of restrictive practices growing out of the
casual system. The Committee had received additional stimu-
lation when, on November 9, the Minister of Labour's earlier
expression of Government determination to press ahead with
the implementation of the Devlin Committee recommendations
was supported by the Prime Minister in the Queen's Speech.
The Prime Minister said the business ahead was considered of
"the highest importance," and left no doubt that the Government would introduce appropriate legislation and take any
other actions needed to achieve decasualization.

While the business of the NMC was considered confidential
it was recognized that at times it would be necessary for the
two sides to refer matters back to their constituents, this to be
done with the concurrence of the Committee. Nevertheless, it
was agreed that dock workers and port employees should be
kept informed of objectives and progress. To accomplish this,
periodic bulletins would be issued. The first was released in
October and mailed to the homes of all dock workers by the
NDLB. In all, six bulletins were issued in this fashion in order
to ensure acceptance once a plan was ready.[21]

---

[21]National Modernization Committee, *Docks Bulletin*, no. 1; "Welfare
Amenities," no. 2; "Dock Labour Scheme," no. 3; "Sick Pay Scheme,"
no. 4; "D Day in the Docks," no. 5; "Statement from the Independent
Members of the National Modernization Committee," no. 6.

Progress of Decasualization

By the end of the year, negotiations over the national issues had progressed to the point where local ones could be undertaken. The NJC, therefore, in December invited the local joint committees in the various ports to appoint local modernization committees which they did. The London Local Modernization Committee was comprised of fifteen representatives of labor. The TGWU named eight from the docks, four of whom were lay members (two each from the Ocean and Riverside groups) and four were officers. The other union members were representatives of the OST Clerks, the NASD, and the Lightermen. There were also employers representing the various divisions in the industry. Because of the large size of this committee, smaller modernization committees were also created, one for the Enclosed Docks, including the PLA; the others for the Riverside, the OST Clerks, and the Lightermen. It is particularly to be noted, because of a subsequent development, that the No. 1 Docks Group Committee of the TGWU was not formally represented on these committees. However, four men holding seats on the No. 1 Docks Group Committee also were among those seated on the London Modernization Committee, at least in 1969 and 1970. Progress was slow as the local negotiators proceeded to negotiate local working arrangements. Throughout 1966 and 1967, up to the institution of decasualization, so much discussion, much of it tantalizing, had never before been known and never before were unions and employers in the industry so deeply enmeshed with Government departments and legislation. A complicated mosaic of developments provided the background of, and the supplementation to, the industrial negotiations.

In summary, on the one hand, there were the industrial organizations and the joint machinery in the industry; alongside of this was the National Dock Labour Scheme, and, not least, the Government, functioning largely through the Ministries of Labour and Transport. The latter had launched the Rochdale Committee (pp. 5, 7 above) and when the industrial machinery concurrently produced the Crichton-Cousins Accord, only to run into a stalemate in negotiations, the Ministry of

Labour launched the Devlin Committee and its important report followed. Out of it all emerged the National Policy Directive and the creation of the national and local modernization committees which tackled the negotiable problems of wages structure, sick pay, pensions, severance, and restrictive practices. From the ministries, but with active involvement of the parties to the industrial machinery, came the necessary legislation, the Docks and Harbours Act, which provided for the licensing of employers, and the Amendment of the National Dock Labour Scheme, which set the mechanics, guidelines, and controls for decasualization. The NDLB was assigned the task of surveying amenities and promoting improvements. Concurrently, with amendment of the Dock Labour Scheme, the industrial machinery produced the all-important "provisional" agreement. Altogether, these steps constituted Devlin Stage I, leading to Decasualization Day, and set the stage for Devlin Stage II.

Of four areas of action — negotiations, welfare and amenities, licensing of employers, amendment of the National Dock Labour Scheme — negotiations were, without doubt, the core. The others, though important, were basically supplemental. The NDLB promptly approved and issued standards for amenities; that is, sanitary conveniences, washing, cloakrooms, canteens, and messroom facilities. Licenses of employers, and the renewal of licenses, were to be based on adequate compliance, but this was not simple and the role of employers became tenuous, with all the uncertainties ahead. Which employers would survive and be licensed? Would nationalization, the prospect of which was looming conspicuously, knock out private employers? Anyway, voluntary amalgamations and mergers of employers began to take place as consolidations into various consortia were made in order to introduce the new technology and manage the expected requirements of decasualization. Legislation was needed to provide for licensing of employers, and the National Dock Labour Scheme had to be amended.

Regarding licensing, the Ministry of Transport issued a statement on transport policy in July 1966, which gave as the main purpose of licensing employers the need "to bring about a large-scale reduction in the number...so as to eliminate the casual employer and reduce the present excessive fragmentation of responsibility."[22] Later, the Docks and Harbours Act of 1966, receiving royal assent in August, officially provided for licensing of employers.[23]

No major opposition to the principle of licensing existed. The NAPE was convinced that placing on the individual employer the cost of maintaining a regular labor force, rather than relying on a pool of labor maintained by the NDLB, would itself eliminate the more casual employers. At the same time, it accepted licensing in order to achieve consolidation on the scale and with the speed necessary to enable a satisfactory system of regular employment to be introduced.

Controversy over identity of the licensing authority developed, however. The Devlin Committee had recommended that the National Ports Council, a body that had been established much earlier to work out plans for port development and operation, be entrusted with the authority and responsibility for licensing. But, the Dock and Harbour Authorities Association argued that the port authority in each port should be designated. In discussions with the Minister of Labour, the Minister of Transport, and the interested parties, the NAPE reiterated the objection raised by the Devlin Committee that the port authorities, which — in some instances — were operational employers, would be involved in a conflict of interest in licensing their competitors. But the National Ports Council did not want the assignment. In light of counterarguments, the Government designated the port authorities as the licensing agent, subject to an applicant's right of appeal to the Minister of Transport. The port authorities, particularly the Port of London Authority, apparently "leaned over backward" in the licensing process to make sure no charge could be held against them.

---

[22]Ministry of Transport, *Transport Policy* (London: Her Majesty's Stationery Office, Cmnd. 3057, 1966), p. 26.

[23]*Docks and Harbours Act 1966, Chapter 28* (London: Her Majesty's Stationery Office, 1966).

As early as November of 1965, a subcommittee of the NJC, in conjunction with officials of the Ministry of Labour and representatives of the NDLB, had formulated proposals for amending the National Dock Labour Scheme, in accordance with the recommendations of the Devlin Committee. After consultation with the NMC and with its approval, the Minister of Labour published a Draft Order on March 25, 1966, amending the National Dock Labour Scheme and appointed Sir George Honeyman, Q.C., to conduct an inquiry and report. The inquiry was held in June, the report issued in August.[24] It laid the necessary groundwork for the subsequent legislation which would amend the National Dock Labour Scheme looking toward decasualization.

Meanwhile, negotiations — both local and national — were conducted simultaneously in an interrelated way on the four subjects originally tackled at the national level: wages structure and levels, sick pay plans, improvement of pensions, and elimination of restrictive practices, each important in its own right.

Wage Dispute — Devlin Again

The negotiations and dispute over wages incident to decasualization reveal the complexities and the difficulties which the parties had to face.[25] It was not alone an ordinary wage claim, an adjustment was to be made, on the one hand, as a consequence of the introduction of regular employment and, on the other, in consideration of the abolition of restrictive practices which had resulted from casual employment, particularly with respect to restrictions on mobility and unreasonable restrictions on overtime working. It was readily agreed that the employer had an obligation to pay any worker for whom no work could be found at a full daily rate, rather than by means

---

[24]Ministry of Labour, *Report of Inquiry held under Paragraph 5 of the Schedule to the Dock Workers (Regulation of Employment) Act, 1946* (London: Her Majesty's Stationery Office, 1966).

[25]This section is based in large part upon *Report of the Committee of Inquiry under Lord Devlin into the Wages Structure and Level of Pay for Dock Workers* (London: Her Majesty's Stationery Office, Cmnd. 3104, 1960).

of attendance money or fall-back guarantee. The employers accepted an obligation to provide a uniform sick pay scheme and an improved pension scheme — although the amounts and forms of payments were being negotiated separately and presented their own difficulties. These were recognized as imposing substantial costs upon employers and the question of wages could not be settled without relationship to them.

Overtime payments and practices were also tied in with the question of what could be done with wages. Restrictions upon working overtime were costly to employers; if they could be removed, the question of wages could be considered differently. The employers had in mind the elimination of practices such as the following: (1) refusal to work overtime on subsequent days, unless overtime was worked on a ship's first day; (2) refusal, when a weekend intervened, to work overtime on weekdays unless overtime was also called for on Saturday and Sunday; (3) refusal to work overtime unless all gangs were ordered out; (4) refusal to work overtime unless penalty payments were made — for example, the requirement that any work done after 5 P.M. would carry a minimum overtime pay of four hours. But the wages structure had to be considered first.

When the parties reached a stalemate in April 1966, Lord Devlin was appointed again as chairman of a board of inquiry to seek a solution to the problem. Hearings were held in May and June. The committee received representatives of the parties but also availed itself of the services of consultants appointed by the Minister of Labour. But, by this time, the trade unions were asking for a guarantee of £ 17 per week.

It was found that neither side was interested in a straight guaranteed wage. The trade unions wanted guaranteed employment and preferred to press for a high basic wage with continuation of piece rates. The basic time rate currently was only about half average earnings. Employers, for the most part, feared the possible "disincentive" effect of a high basic wage. All wanted a moderate basic wage and most wanted to institute a bonus in place of piece rates, although Riverside employers generally were willing to retain piece rates. The result was that the parties looked at structure differently and were confronted as well with a considerable gap between proposed basic rates.

Any rate above the going time rate would have given some additional protection against, or mitigated the effects of, individual misfortune or occasional hard times. The unions were looking for as much security as possible, but, if the increase were not much above the going time rate and substantially below the average rate of earnings, it would have offered little to the majority of the men. If a man expected to earn double the basic guarantee, how much interest would he have in a guarantee? A substantial payment, on the other hand, would not have been covered by any immediate increase in productivity, although regular employment would have produced immediate savings in time wasted in hiring under the old system. Time consumed in the "free call" and in allocation of men after daily hiring was significant. This would be saved. Flexibility in the use of men would make further savings. But not all savings were to be immediate. The employers pointed out that during the first year, at least, they would be operating with an excessive labor force inflated by conditions of the casual market, the size of which would only gradually be reduced by natural wastage and retirements even though some retirements could be induced by improved pensions.

An anomaly in the situation was that the trade unions had long sought the reform. Having sought it, why were they asking for such a large down payment? As the Devlin Committee put this point, "If the employers are at last prepared to concede it [decasualization] why should the men expect to be paid for accepting it?"

Nevertheless, the employers accepted the principle that the men had a right to share in savings to be made under the new scheme. Their concern was the amount of the initial "investment." They knew they had to overcome any feeling the men might have — valid or not — that there was more in it for the employers than for them. The employers knew they had to purchase good will. Probably they also knew that if they refused to pay anything until after they knew exactly what they were going to get in exchange, they might not get anything at all. They knew they had to make an advance payment, because their choice was between modernization and leaving the industry as it was. The trade union side wanted the payment as an increase on the wage; the employers wanted to make a modernization payment. The employers proposed a bonus payment of so much per hour to all workers at work or available for work. They would not give percentage increases on existing rates. Further, all earnings, except weekend earnings, were to be offset against the guarantee.

In 1966, the trade union side was seeking a weekly guarantee of £ 17. The employers wanted one of £ 14, but were willing to offer a London differential of £ 1. All earnings, except weekend earnings would be offset against the guarantee. The guarantee would be conditional upon fulfillment of the dock worker's obligations, including reasonable overtime during the week. Considering everything, the parties were far from agreement.

Devlin thought the employers had gone about as far as they could go, yet observed that "they seem [ed] genuinely determined that [decasualization should] not fail through their unwillingness to take a chance on the future." He was convinced that the union leaders, in bargaining style, had set their sights high — because there were no established principles to show how a claim should be judged — and presented their case as firmly as they could to see what they could get.

The unavoidable fact in the situation was that when the trade union leaders presented the idea of a modernization payment to the men, they got a very strong unfavorable response. The employers' plan was criticized on the ground that it was making the wage structure more complicated, that it would be a disincentive to the piece worker.[26] The workers also saw it as a throwback to a wartime system which had been unpopular.

---

[26]On the contrary, the piece worker suffered from waste of time under the casual system in a way the time worker did not — maybe more so than the employer.

The Devlin Committee carefully considered whether to invite the employers, notwithstanding the strength of their case, to give way. With the men feeling as they did — even if wholly irrationally — they would not consent and the trade union leaders could not make them. The battle for modernization would be lost before it was won. It was said:

It comes down to this. The virtues of the modernisation payment are that it ensures equality and is flexible in the sense that it leaves the final disposition of the money to be settled in accordance with the new wage structure; by its name it impresses on those who receive it that it is exceptional and is being paid for something out of the ordinary which they have to do in return — in short, that it is a payment for modernisation. The only real objection to it is that it is novel. If this objection is allowed to prevail, what hope is there for modernisation itself? Putting it quite bluntly, if men will not take £ 2 a week extra for changing their habits because payment is offered in a novel form, what hope is there of their changing their habits? If the new settlement follows the usual pattern of a wage increase, there must be a serious danger that the men will feel that everything else is to continue just as before. The employers, who are to pay in advance for a change of habits, can in such circumstances have no assurance that they will get what they are paying for. The employers are paying the money as an earnest of their good intentions to share with the men the benefit of change; they are entitled in return to an earnest from the men of their intention to accept change. A demand that the new settlement should follow the usual pattern of the wage increase is the very negation of change. If the employers accept it, it will mean, and will be widely understood to mean, that everything is to continue just as before.

The Devlin Committee did not want to have a rejection of reform simply because the men disliked the form of payment offered. It concluded that, with the abolishing of attendance money, each man should get a minimum daily wage of 44s and 4d, plus a modernization payment of 40s a week, together with one shilling for every hour of overtime (including week-end working) actually worked. The fall-back payment was to be abolished and to each worker who fulfilled his obligations under the scheme, should his earnings from all sources (excluding weekend work) fall below £ 15, his employer would pay the difference. Also, there should be a London differential of £ 1 per week in the guarantee.

On October 3, 1966, the day the Devlin Committee Report was published, the Minister of Labour called both sides of the NMC to a meeting to tell them of the Government's acceptance, in principle, of the pay changes recommended but conditional on specific agreement for the elimination of restrictive working practices. Also, increases would be governed by the provisions of the Price and Income Policy. On October 10, the Executive Committee of the NAPE accepted the recommendations. The trade unions spent some time explaining the implications of the report to their members. It was not until December 9 that the National Docks Delegates' Conference of the TGWU, by a vote of 57 to 24, accepted the recommendations; and later in the month, they were accepted by the NASD.

While meetings, conferences, and "negotiations" on the Devlin recommendations were going on, leading to the necessary understandings and recommendations preparatory to decasualization, still other complications developed. One of the greatest had come with the announcement in March 1966, in the Labour Party's Election Manifesto, of the Labour Party's intention to nationalize the docks industry. Inasmuch as employers were then working in close consultation with various departments of the Government, they were shocked. It seemed ironical to them that the Government, being one of the parties to the Devlin plan of reform, would countenance such a disruptive announcement. There was even a question among employers whether the Government would continue to support the decasualization program and whether they ought to go forward with negotiations under the circumstances. However, the Prime Minister said that the new dock proposals were not intended to derogate from the urgency of completing current negotiations on decasualization and modernization.

The Question of
Nationalization Reviewed

THE National Executive Committee of the Labour Party, in December 1965, had set up a study group on the port transport industry. Its report had been finished in the following March but was not published until June.[27] The Study Group did not criticize the findings of the Devlin Committee Report but looked upon its recommendations only as "a minimum programme...presented not as an ideal solution or even as the most simple and lasting one, but only as a way of achieving decasualization with the minimum of upset and resistance." This, it said, was not enough. "The wrong kind of decasualization could be even more wasteful of manpower and equipment than the present casual and semi-casual system." A more radical course was needed.

The Study Group had been instructed to look at ownership, organization, and efficiency of British docks in the light

[27]*Report of the Labour Party Study Group on the Port Transport Industry,* Labour Party, June 1966, known as the Mikardo Report, from the chairman of the Study Group.

of the role public enterprise played or could play and the contribution it could make. Although its findings were the usual ones, its conclusions and recommendations differed from those of others which, in the political context of Great Britain, was probably not surprising. The Group's report was critical of the Dock Labour Scheme for regularizing "the casual system by inserting a holding employer, the NDLB, between the operational employer and the employee" and charged that it had "not prevented the maintenance, perhaps even the multiplication, of all the gradations of privilege and preference that divide dock workers." It found "the absence of strong control by the Unions" and "bad labour relations" to be results of the casual system. It found misuse of resources in competition between ports and saw no hope of getting rid of restrictive practices, or of extending shift work, or introducing productivity, unless the workers' insecurity was mitigated. Licensing of employers was not a workable solution of the industry's problem and the work of the NMC could not lead to an effective solution. Public ownership and employee participation were considered requisites. Industrial relations would improve, the NDLB would have no reason for continuing, and "decasualization under one employer would lead to efficient deployment of labour...improved equipment and better use of it, and to the more rapid introduction of new techniques."

It recommended a national ports authority for strategic planning, operation of appropriate common services, supervision of a consistent and rational pricing policy and training program, and cooperation in development of a national transport plan. Regional port authorities would be established to exercise over-all managerial responsibility as the sole operator of cargo handling operations and the sole employer of port transport employees. Local dock labor boards would be continued as joint employer-employee bodies to carry out such functions not disposed of in the move to one employer. At dock level, there would be group operating committees whose main functions would be efficient use of equipment and manpower; resolution of pay and productivity questions not decided at the national level; handling of disciplinary matters, safety, news sheet, training, welfare, and selection of supervisors. But management by committees was not being proposed because "the Manager was to manage."

The Anti-Devlin Report

Along the way came another voice critical of almost everything being contemplated and proposing a still more revolutionary program for immediate implementation, the "Anti-Devlin Report."[28] Disdainful of the Devlin Committee membership and recommendations, the "protracted talks" to implement the Devlin Committee proposals by "the official Union and Employers' representatives, assisted by the Government," and the Government's efforts to facilitate the recommendations by legislative proposals, it asserted that "sharp reactions from the militant unofficial leadership" were developing "powerful and effective assistance, in the forms both of political pressures [lobbying] and strike action" to prevent the introduction of new legislation then being prepared. "Nationalization of the industry" was called for immediately, not the Government's "commitment to 'eventual' nationalization." It was even critical of the Communist Party and Jack Dash, chairman of the unofficial Liaison Committee, whose program, it was alleged, also fell short of workers' control. For itself the claim was made that "this Anti-Devlin Report is the only source of seriously thought out alternatives to both Devlin and orthodox nationalization." The report wanted to inject "a serious demand for a major structural reform in the direction of workers' control" and it charged that "the Government desperately needs a success in the field of rational industry; a successful neo-capitalist design for the docks would be a major triumph. It is of great importance that it should be met with

[28]*An Anti-Devlin Report — The Dockers' Next Step* (no author, publisher, or date). The publication grew out of a discussion in a so-called, special dockers seminar, at what was called the *Week Voice* workers control conference in Manchester in June 1963, and subsequent discussions of similar groups; generally thought to be Trotskyite.

a serious socialist alternative around which workers' aspirations can be mobilized."

In the light of such views, it was naturally critical of the Devlin Committee's program, which stopped short of nationalization and rested on retention of a few private employers, and characterized this as an "odious drive for manipulated servility" and "subservient relations between dockers and employers," the thing, it said, that kept Devlin Committee from recommending nationalization. A move to one employer was the only solution, but not "orthodox nationalization," as the report characterized the type being promoted by the Labour Party. It insisted that decasualization *"as such,* and as seen by employers and Devlin, is *not* a dockers goal and if the dockers have to sacrifice the powers and controls which they have today, the price is too high." On the other hand, it was asserted, "decasualization of earnings is a dockers' goal," whereas "strengthening... employers' powers over workers" is not acceptable. "There is a marked skepticism among dockers about the value of orthodox nationalization...businessmen's syndicalism," it was said. This they did not want.

The alternative suggested was a national port authority with all port installations under public ownership. Hence, the abolition of all private employers of dock labor. The national port authority would be the sole contractor for dock labor, would replace the NAPE, and would bargain with the unions. Central to the proposal was self-management of labor by means of port workers councils elected from the trade unions, with the local councils tied to a national port workers council.

"Steps" toward Nationalization

While negotiations within the local modernization committees were proceeding, a Government White Paper on transport policy was published in July 1966.[29] It explicitly stated that policies regarding port modernization were immediate and necessary steps toward the realization of the Government's in-

---

[29]Ministry of Transport, *Transport Policy.*

tention of reorganizing the ports on the basis of public own-ership. To this end, there was projected the need to create a strong national ports authority and several regional port authorities. No indication of the timing of such an event was then given, but following publication of the report of the Honeyman Inquiry (p. 25) on amendment of the National Dock Labour Scheme and the wage report of the recent Devlin Committee, the Government made known its intention of intro-ducing legislation in the 1968–1969 session of Parliament, with the expectation that nationalization would come into effect in 1970.

In spite of forewarnings by earlier pronouncements this was disconcerting to employers who found formal announce-ment of intentions to nationalize the industry to be at odds with the Government's active role in pressing for decasual-ization of employment. The Government, however, kept up its pressure. Nor were employers prepared to resist, for they had concluded that decasualization was essential regardless. Decasualization was imperative for modernization and if they balked on decasualization it probably would have speeded nationalization. They were, of course, concerned about costs of decasualization which they could not recover unless reim-bursed by the Government.

It might be noted that nationalization was not such a strange prospect; uncertainties concerned what would be nationalized. Actually, nationalization of port facilities would not have been all that difficult to take if it ended there. It would not have changed very much, in light of the four types of ports in England. First, there were the trust ports or authorities set up by private act of Parliament to further the public interest through development of port facilities. These were not all alike and varied in functions; the Mersey Docks and Harbour Board, for example, owned and controlled all the port facili-ties, while the Port of London Authority owned and controlled some port facilities but also performed stevedoring in com-petition with private companies. Second, there were ports which were already nationalized. These originally were the railroad ports and when the railroads were nationalized they, too, were nationalized, but were spun off and governed by a special docks board. Third, there were private ports or ports with private facilities. In some places, like London, private port facilities existed along side of facilities of the port authority. Fourth, there were municipal ports, like Southampton and Hull. Nationalization, of course, could extend to all ports or only to a limited number. But would the labor force be nationalized?

The TGWU was committed to nationalization both of facilities and of the labor force. So were the NASD and the Lightermen. The Government would be the sole employer and would do the loading and discharging. But nationalization could reach to ownership of shipping, too, although no one was suggesting this. As a matter of fact, there were those in the labor movement, including leaders in the docks unions, who thought that the proposals on nationalization of the docks were half-baked, that the Mikardo "investigation" was rushed through without time for members of the committee really to understand all of the problems of the industry. In any case, the prospect of nationalization was so disconcerting to many employers that the issue would be alive at the point when decasualization was introduced.

The employers submitted their objections, contending that objectives of unified control of policy and planning could be achieved without nationalization by converting the National Ports Council into a national ports authority, as originally recommended in the Rochdale Report, and that there was no valid operational reason for regional port authorities. The high degree of union employer collaboration and cooperation should continue, but, unlike the unions, they saw no future for the NDLB whose functions could be integrated into the national ports authority. They also pointed out that the many areas of uncertainty about the Government's intentions were grave detriments to future planning.

A further step toward nationalization of the docks industry took place in July 1967, when the Minister of Transport, Barbara Castle, issued a memorandum on the subject.[30] The memorandum was intended as further explication of the policy of the Government as presented in the White Paper on Transport Policy delivered to Parliament the previous July. Nationalization was deemed more urgent because of the impact of the container revolution, the technological change that was leading to the use of huge cargo containers hoisted on and off ships by mechanical equipment, which was gathering pace rapidly. It reaffirmed need for unified control through a national ports authority, supplemented by a limited number of regional authorities. The organization and duties of these bodies were specified in some detail, but only the larger and more significant ports were to be included in the initial scheme. Various nonstatutory undertakings were to be continued but the line of demarcation was not explicit. Further, although regional port authorities were to consult with the unions to establish and maintain machinery for negotiations at all levels, the extent and form of worker participation were to be left to the industry to work out. Several alternate forms of worker participation were, however, mentioned without commitment. The local dock labor boards might or might not be continued. The functions delegated to these bodies under the amended National Dock Labour Scheme — that is, responsibilities for temporary transfers of workers from one employer to another, the control of the register, discipline, training, and welfare and amenities — would be taken care of in whatever fashion the arrangements for worker participation took. Finally, the vesting date was set for January 1, 1970, if the legislation were introduced in the 1968–1969 session of Parliament.

---

[30] "Ports Reorganization," mimeo.

Decasualization - Devlin Stage I

PRESSURE developed from within the trade unions as the spring of 1967 wore on, particularly among the tally clerks in London, for an early announcement of the date when decasualization would be consummated.[31] Consequently, when the independent members of the NMC informed the Minister of Labour that progress in negotiations warranted an announcement, he responded — politically — on June 1 saying that decasualization would be introduced no later than mid-September. In retrospect, it seems proper to remark that the beginning was rushed.[32]

It was perhaps necessary to force the matter, but there were many reasons why the time was not propitious for inaugurating

---

[31]It is interesting and ironical that a decasualization agreement for tally clerks had been negotiated early in 1965 but was not effectuated because of the opposition of one of the branches of tally clerks in the NASD.

[32]*The Port,* Jan. 30, 1969, contains a poignant remark to this effect from one of the TGWU leaders. "There is no doubt in my mind," he says, "that the tally clerks stampeded the Minister of Labour into introducing decasualization when he did." Many employers shared such feelings from the beginning because certain problems had not been resolved.

decasualization. The Minister of Labour himself was under the policy of "severe restraint," administered by the Income and Prices Board, which caused him to be inflexible on wage increases, unless covered by real productivity. Increased productivity was in prospect but only immediate wage adjustments would satisfy the men. Employer licensing complaints, dealing mostly with the numbers of men to be allocated to given employers, had not been settled. The problem of labor surplus to employers and fear of redundancy on the part of the men were of critical importance. Equally important, the making of allocations in accordance with preferences expressed by the men and individual companies, in light of the expected needs in different sectors and among various employers — adjusting supply with all of the expressed preferences to *demand,* divided, as it was, among employers by sectors — was inevitably a gargantuan task.

There was not enough time to do the job. The financing of decasualization had not been completely determined. If employers made outlays, would they be given an opportunity to recover them, particularly under the prospect of nationalization? Employers wanted increases in cargo-handling charges, in any event (and in this they were to be thwarted). Differences between the TGWU and the NASD had not been resolved and the question of a common register in London had not been settled. But the Minister of Labour was determined to go ahead. He had to ask the Cabinet for a specific date, which he got, and he had to lay before Parliament the bill to amend the Dock Labour Scheme, which he did.

Amended National Dock Labour Scheme

The amendment of the National Dock Labour Scheme was passed in mid-August, to come into operation on September 18, 1967.[33] The NDLB and the local dock labor boards were continued, the object of the Scheme being to ensure dock work-

---

[33]*The Dock Workers (Regulation of Employment) (Amendment) Order 1967.* Statutory Instruments, 1967, no. 1252; cf. National Dock Labour Board, *The Dock Workers Employment Scheme,* 1967.

ers of greater regularity of employment and management of enough workers for efficient performance. The Board was to continue to control the register and recruitment. It was assigned the task of allocating the men to licensed employers. If an employer quit the industry his men were to return to the Board and be reallocated. The local boards were to supervise temporary transfers of workers between employers to meet day-to-day fluctuations in demand; but workers were expected to work for their own employers at least 80 percent of the time. In addition, the local boards were to serve as appeal bodies and administer programs collective in scope; that is, holidays, pension and sickness plans.

Both employers and workers were deemed to have accepted the obligations of the Scheme. All workers were put into permanent engagement and no worker could be terminated without consent of the local board and the worker was given a right to appeal to a local tribunal. An employer could discipline workers for up to five days without pay, with the worker having the right to appeal to the local board. The employer could dismiss a worker for serious misconduct, but the individual was to remain in the employment of the local board while a decision was being made. If the dismissal was found to be unjustifiable, the worker could be reinstated without loss of pay. If the dismissal were upheld the worker was given a right to appeal to the local appeals tribunal.

The task of allocation of the men went on apace for the month preceding September 18. It was a night and day job. A total of 23,500 men had to be absorbed, although approximately 10,000 were already in weekly engagement. This meant that 13,500 had to be allocated. All employers had been asked to show the number of different categories of men, both daily and weekly, actually employed on each normal working day from July 1, 1964 to June 30, 1965. Both employers and workers were allowed to list their preferences for each other. Although 65 percent were allocated on the basis of their choices, some serious social problems were created by the other assignments. Some had to be allocated against their wishes, even to other sectors. A man of long residence in one sector, for example, who was not a steady employee of a particular employer, but who had found good employment by shifting about, because he was recognized as a good worker, found himself assigned out of a sector, while a younger man was not so assigned because he had regularly worked for a given employer in the prior six months. Challenges by men of their assignments and by employers of numbers allocated to them had not all been resolved.

The "Provisional" National Agreement

With decasualization approaching, the parties pressed on to complete negotiations for a new national agreement. Consensus was achieved on all terms, except one which later became the center of a major difficulty. Because of this one point of difference the agreement was characterized as a provisional agreement, although it became operative in all other respects.[34]

This agreement, to become effective with the advent of permanent employment on September 18, 1967, provided that a dock worker available for eight full hours of work was to receive a minimum daily wage and a modernization payment. A dock worker who was available for work on each of five normal working days, and who fulfilled his obligations under the National Dock Labour Scheme, was guaranteed a payment of £ 15 for that week. London was to have a £ 1 differential. (These were the wages recommended by the Devlin Committee but, subsequently, employers in London had agreed to a £ 17 wage.) If he was unavailable on any week day, a man's guarantee was reduced accordingly. All earnings in the normal work week were to count against the guarantee. Practices of the casual system of employment, such as restrictions on mobility within working periods, whether between different points or between different operations, were to be eliminated.

---

[34]National Joint Council for the Port Transport Industry, "Provisional Agreement between the National Association of Port Employers on Behalf of its Members in the Transport and General Workers Union on its Own Behalf and on Behalf of the Union's Associated with it Specified in the Schedule Hereto," Sept. 15, 1967, mimeo.

The unions were not willing to accept the following proposition:

Where a dockworker is unable to work because of a stoppage of work by other port workers due to a trade dispute, the employer may suspend his employment forthwith, provided that he shall be paid a guaranteed weekly payment break for the first week of such suspension.

Previously, under the casual system, it had been customary for the workers to return to the NDLB and be reallocated or paid attendance money. Under the new system of permanent employment, the wage to be received by the men was much greater, and the employers thought it would be financially crippling to carry employees idled because of a strike. The total agreement became provisional because this proposition of the employers was completely unacceptable to the unions.

The problem of the employers, as the day for decasualization approached, was making sure that the costs of the guarantee would be covered. The expectation right along had been to offset the cost of decasualization by cooperation in eliminating restrictive practices and through greater mobility and efficiency. Mobility and efficiency were only prospective; therefore, the employers sought immediate increases in charges for handling cargoes. However, when the PLA announced a 20 percent increase for unloading, the Government intervened to block it.

The Common Register and Related Questions

As the scheduled date for decasualization approached, the question of the common register was a most important problem in London. To the employers the common register was an essential prerequisite to decasualization, and three courses appeared to be open to them: refuse to implement weekly employment until the common register was accepted (but this would have been contrary to the statute and would have produced a national strike); accept the current "continuity rules" and hope that a common register would be agreed to later (but this would have meant that on occasions an employer might have to pay stevedores, for example, for standing by, while dockers were borrowed to do the work); or avoid mixing men from the two unions on the same work, but, where mixing was unavoidable, to insist at the end of the day that they had to return and continue to work together (whereas the old "continuity rules" would not have compelled a return to mixed working on a second day). The consensus emerged among the Ocean Traders in London that they should operate as if the common register existed, that they should stand firm for it, but that they should endeavor to place the right men in the right work. The continuity rules, as will be seen, however, were to cause trouble. The problem, of course, was one of mobility and flexibility.

The Dock Labour Board in London always had carried all registered dock workers upon a single main register, which, in turn, was divided into three subregisters, one for dockers, one for tally clerks, and one for lightermen. Theoretically, the Board made no distinction between men in the TGWU and those in the NASD. Both were included in the same subregister. But, in practice, the men were identifiable and allocations had conformed wherever possible to the traditional demarcations of work between the two groups. Whenever it was not possible, men still had to be allocated but had remained on such assignments only during the day in accord with the continuity rules.

Obviously, the demand of the employers for a common register was more than a demand for a common listing. In a sense there was already a common register, and it should be noted that "common register" was in a sense a misnomer. What was sought was the abolition of the demarcation between the work of dockers and stevedores, the elimination of any system of differentiation. To the employers this was essential to effective decasualization and was necessary to achieve the expected mobility and flexibility.

There had been correspondence and meetings between the two unions over the question of establishing a common register in this sense, once decasualization was introduced. As early as February 1966, the leaders had agreed in principle to it. They had scheduled a meeting to work out the mechanics of making all work available to all members, but it never convened. It may have been that when employers in March called attention to forthcoming developments involving port changes designed to accommodate new technology, the men were alarmed about loss of work. It was known that members of NASD were very sensitive to suggestions of losing or sharing ship work. The employers felt they had to be neutral while the two unions worked out an agreement, yet, to them, to perpetuate demarcation would cause immense complications for attainment of full decasualization. But union representatives had stated that they personally thought the elimination of demarcation would benefit all concerned in the industry. Further joint meetings were planned but, like the former ones, they did not come off. The two unions seemed to move to stickier and stickier positions, notwithstanding that leaders in both kept saying that the men would accept the changes contemplated.[35] The notion of a common register was rejected by the NASD as late as August 20, when it failed of ratification by a small majority. Actually, the problem was not resolved until decasualization was in effect.

---

[35]A precursor to the trouble to come had developed in the late spring of 1966 when freight loaded and discharged for Fred Olson Limited was transferred from the Canary Wharf, West Indies Dock, where it had always been performed by docker members of the TGWU, to the modern building at "P" Shed, Millwall Dock. The dockers expected to follow the work while the stevedores claimed all ship work. The details of the dispute need no elaboration. It was not settled within the industrial machinery in London and, in the course of events, it went to the NJC, which ultimately placed it before an arbitration panel. But after a unanimous recommendation that the work was TGWU work, because it was work being transferred within the sector, the "blues" reaffirmed their decision to do all ship work. At this juncture, a Court of Inquiry was established and the complicated issue was carefully outlined. *Report of a Court of Inquiry into the causes and circumstances of a Strike by members of the National Amalgamated Stevedores and Dockers in the Port of London, and into practices relevant thereto* (London: Her Majesty's Stationery Office, Cmnd. 3146, 1966), pp. 8–9. Referred to as the Wilson Court of Inquiry.

There also remained the still unresolved problem of adjustment of the size of the register. In January 1967, it was estimated that surplus labor would take from three to five years to waste away and that by that time there would be a new surplus resulting from the introduction of palletization, unitization, and containerization. Consequently, the employers needed a plan to reduce the number of men. They had repeatedly given assurances that no one would be declared redundant but planned reduction had to be achieved. Proposals for compulsory retirement had been discussed in May and June. The NAPE proposals were rejected at the National Docks Delegate Conference on August 1. Both sides met with the Minister of Labour on August 18, the day amendment of the Dock Labour Scheme was presented to Parliament. The employers thought failure of agreement on compulsory retirement necessitated delay of inauguration of decasualization but the Minister of Labour did not share the view. When no further progress was made, employers went ahead with a modest voluntary retirement scheme, but pensions and severance plans would still involve much negotiation.

Working literally almost around the clock, the allocation of the men was achieved by September 15, but there were many complaints and no time to resolve them. More ominous was the uncertainty about what the opponents of decasualization might do, or be able to do. Opposition came from two main sources. Men who preferred the opportunities of the casual system, particularly those who had established themselves as good earners and were able to enjoy preferences in hiring, saw a loss in weekly earnings. This was a real, not a fancied, prospect, notwithstanding that the vast majority stood to gain in one way or another. Then there were those who had political motives of one sort or another. Despite all efforts, decasualization had not been completely sold.

Few anticipated the magnitude of the trouble ahead, although some trouble was expected; "teething troubles," was their term. In answer to speculations immediately prior to decasualization, Mr. Gunter, the Minister of Labour, speaking of the possibility of a strike, said he expected Jack Dash and the unofficial Liaison Committee to make a "pretty massive campaign over the weekend," but he assured the public that the TGWU had done much to "diminish the influence of the unofficial elements. The effectiveness of these elements has diminished over the past few weeks. . . . What their success will be tomorrow, I don't know. But I am hopeful, reinforced by what has happened over the past few weeks, and speaking from some personal experience, that the men are not so willing to be led astray. There will be some carefully planned attempts to undermine the union position. But I am satisfied now that the vast majority of dockers will recognize that the new system represents a tremendous advance towards better conditions, although there are some further points for negotiation." He also said there were "encouraging signs" because he felt the men were largely satisfied that their interests were best served by sticking to their unions.[36] Perhaps apprehensively, he added, "It would be the irony of ironies of industrial history if, having striven for so long to bring good conditions to dockland, men followed unofficial leadership and declined to follow the guidance of their negotiators."[37]

Decasualization Day

The historic day of September 18, 1967, the date set for complete decasualization of all dock work, dawned in London under leaden skies. A heavy downpour of rain added to the difficulty of effectuating the new program. Jack Dash was at the Royal Docks, as was expected, haranguing the men and calling for a strike. How many were following him and the unofficial Liaison Committee was not immediately clear because the rain curtailed most operations.

At the outset, employers were relieved that the strike had been confined mainly to Tilbury and the Royal Docks. Men in the Tooley Street area, who had struck over dissatisfaction with allocations, were quickly satisfied that acceptable adjust-

[36]*Daily Telegraph*, Sept. 15, 1967, p. 25.
[37]*Observer*, Sept. 17, 1967, p. 2; *Sunday Times*, Sept. 17, 1967, p. 1.

ments could be made. In the following days it was reported that to all intents and purposes the port was working normally. This was hardly true, for some men seemed intent on holding out. The common view, however, was that the odds on a lengthy strike were never very great. It was heartening to many that the unofficial leaders had not really achieved the support they had hoped for. An important fact was that the employers were not implementing all aspects of the "provisional" agreement, particularly the mobility clauses, not wishing to "rock the boat" at the outset of decasualization. Top union leaders seemed happy, if harassed. "The militants have no more nor less success than we expected. What our men must realize is there's nothing to be won in this. Whoever is responsible for bringing them out will have to answer to the men when they go back for they won't achieve anything." It was hoped that the men would "see sense in a day or two."[38]

In the midst of the confusion of the strike the two unions, the TGWU and the NASD, jointly met on Monday, September 25, within a week of the beginning of decasualization, and agreed to permit the implementation of the common register on Monday, October 2. At the same time, however, the employers still studiously avoided implementing the mobility clauses of the "provisional" agreement, fearing trouble over changes in work-rule practices related to so-called continuity. These clauses, as will be shortly seen, became a major factor in prolonging the stoppage.

The strikers in London were calling for a weekly guarantee of £ 17, instead of £ 16, better sick pay and pensions, and a guarantee that no dockers would be declared redundant. The latter had been promised many times. Sick pay and pensions would require much negotiation. The employers previously had agreed to £ 17, only to have the Minister of Labour refuse to approve it on the advice of the Prices and Incomes Board. These demands were not very meaningful to many of the men. In spite of attempts to spread the strike, there was, by the beginning of the second week, a very substantial acceptance

---

[38]*Financial Times,* Sept. 19, 1967, p. 15.

of work in London. In Liverpool, the other major strike center, the principal cause of the strike was ostensibly the claim for parity with London, crystallizing later into dissatisfaction with piece rates. This quickly became the major dispute, some in London claiming support of the Liverpool dockers as their reason for staying out. The strike in Liverpool ran on for six weeks.

"Second" Stoppage in London — Issues and Problems

In London, not long after the common register officially went into effect on October 2, a new, and more massive, strike action occurred in the Royal Docks over continuity of work. When stevedores, who were loaned to T. Wallis, Ltd., were told to report to their own employer after working for a day, they refused. The orders to return to their own employers had been given under the new agreement but were in conflict with the old displaced continuity rule. Large numbers stayed away from work. As in previous unofficial stoppages, the officials of the unions were unable to control their members and appeared content only to try to discredit the unofficial leaders. The strike in London now overshadowed the one in Liverpool and ran on after the Liverpool strike was settled.

During the course of the unofficial strike, employers in London were confronted with a very serious problem. Due to the strike a large number of men who were willing to work were not able to do so. They, of course, reported for work and were being paid the new guarantee. This was proving to be quite a burden and, from the employers' point of view, quite unjustifiable. But they had not won their point in negotiations that they be excused from payment of the guarantee in the event of idleness due to a strike. There was, however, in the Dock Workers Regulation of Employment Order, a so-called "break clause." It read: "A registered dock worker shall not leave his employment with the National Board or with a registered employer...except by giving not less than seven days' notice...." Feeling the pinch, employers considered invoking the clause to allow an employer to give one week's notice to men on strike, and to others unable to work because of the strike. Caution led to careful consideration both of the probable effects and of whether the clause could be implemented to this end legally.[39] More cautious employers suggested thinking twice before invoking the clause, for in their estimation it would surely broaden the strike and produce a far worse situation. Despite the mounting cost of payments to idle men, the majority felt it inadvisable to aggravate the situation, but debate on the matter continued for some time.

In mid-October, despite doubt that it could be carried off, the proposal that actual strikers be given an ultimatum to return to work or be dismissed gained support. The employers demanded that the Minister of Labour promise to introduce legislation to deal with men taking part in unofficial strikes. The Minister was not prepared to introduce legislation. Following the meeting and after further discussion, the threat was dissipated, the consensus being that to send out dismissal letters might jeopardize the future possibility of amending the Dock Labour Scheme. But the issue could not be kept at rest beneath the crunching cost of paying men in idleness.

---

[39]The Dock Workers Scheme gave the dock workers more protection against unemployment and dismissal than was given by law to any other workers. English law, unlike that in many of the continental countries, had left dismissal entirely at the whim of the employer, checked only by the strength of the union. But in 1963, in the Contracts of Employment Act, minimum periods of notice were laid down. In the Redundancy Payments Acts, of 1965, employers were required to make redundancy payments to dismissed employees, unless they could show that there was no connection with redundancy. While this reduced the employer's power to dismiss as he pleased, insofar as summary dismissal was concerned these two acts left this matter unchanged. Hence, if an employee broke a basic term of his contract his employer was not bound to give notice.

The dock employer, however, was subject to the Local Dock Labour Board regarding dismissals. He had to use the permanent workers who were allocated to him, and he could only transfer them on loan with the approval of the Board. A permanent dock worker was entitled to minimum periods of notice and, if the employer wanted to give notice, he could only do so with the consent of the Local Board. Also, if a dock worker was summarily dismissed because of misconduct, his dismissal had to be investigated by the Local Board before it would be final.

The fact is that employers were not of one mind. The argument was increasingly expressed that notices of dismissal to the unofficial strikers were a necessary prelude to the layoff of those made idle by the strike. Drafts of letters were readied, but the PLA was not inclined to send out notices to those of its employees on strike. This alone was enough to check this move. There were two points of view, one that letters would be ineffective and make little difference and most likely would extend the strike port-wide; the other that employers must at least be seen as doing something. The majority of the Ocean Traders later decided to send dismissal notices (1) if the PLA would change its mind and do likewise, (2) if the Minister of Labour were notified, and (3) if it could be done without jeopardizing the long-term policy of securing an amendment to the Dock Labour Scheme. But the matter was again deferred until unanimity of all employers could be achieved, inasmuch as it was considered damaging if employers seemed to be divided. It was realized, too, that when dismissed men returned to the Dock Labour Board there was little likelihood that they would be disciplined in any way, because it was painfully apparent that the Board then, as in the past, was incapable of administering mass discipline. Furthermore, the leaders of the unions had urgently requested the employers not to try to exercise their right to return men to the Dock Labour Board.

Early in November, the Ocean Traders did send a different type of letter, an open letter, to all dock workers and to the press, pointing out that every man on unofficial strike had lost a considerable sum and those idled by it had lost, too, in spite of the guarantee of £ 16 a week, and that cargoes were being diverted and the country suffering. The letter noted that each docker had had his copy of the "Grey Book" (the Enclosed Docks Agreement) since June, and that they all had a definite employer to whom questions could be put, a good resource for finding out for themselves the answers to any queries they had. They were not dependent upon the unofficial element for information about problems. They were told directly that "the militants want to keep the industry casual...

they do not want better conditions of pay and work...if they did there would be no unofficial strike today." They were also assured that "the employers cannot and will not let their new permanent employees down. They cannot be a party to turning the clock back."[40]

An attempt to clarify the new arrangements regarding continuity was made early in November in another letter to all workers, which pointed out that when workers were in their own sector, except when there happened to be shortages, the continuity arrangements were being maintained substantially as before. The new clauses applied only when men were temporarily transferred to another employer and were designed to provide a dock worker with the maximum amount of work with his own employer or within his own sector. Both the unions and the employers felt, it was noted, that this would provide the only basis upon which good employee-employer relationships could be developed; that is, personal relationships between men and employers could not be established if men were compelled to work continuity with other employers. It was stated, with emphasis, that there was no possibility whatever of the employers giving way to the unofficial Liaison Committee's demands. The written and signed agreement had to stand, although the employers were willing to meet with accredited representatives to discuss and clarify any problems and misunderstandings once the unofficial strike was ended.[41]

On November 10, 1967, a joint committee of representatives from the TGWU and the NASD (which had been in constant session throughout the dispute trying to resolve misunderstandings about continuity) issued a statement to all dock workers, knowing that many of the men wanted the agreement amended so that men on transfer would be given noncontinuity work, but if placed on continuity work, they would then stay on it until completion. With this in mind, the committee pointed out that while the officials of the unions who had met with the em-

---

[40]Open Letter, London Ocean Trades Employers Association, to all dock workers, undated, but about Nov. 1, 1967.

[41]Letter, British Shipping Federation, Ltd., to all workers, Nov. 1, 1967.

ployers found them, as always, not prepared to negotiate while men were on strike, the employers did agree to discuss the following propositions immediately upon full resumption of normal work:

(1) That...priority be given wherever practical to placing men, being transferred between companies, into noncontinuity work.

(2) That, if an employer had to man a complete ship with men transferred from another employer, consideration should be given to the ship being transferred.

(3) That a joint committee be set up of trade unionists and employers to go anywhere in the Enclosed Docks to conciliate on any problem arising from the Grey Book with full authority to make decisions on the spot.

(4) That action be taken against employers who blatantly misuse the agreement.

All men were urged to resume normal work and to allow the constitutional machinery to operate, being assured that union delegates were endeavoring to resolve the current problems. It was promised, in addition, that shop stewards were to be elected throughout the port as soon as there was normal resumption of work.[42]

The unofficial Liaison Committee quickly prepared a mimeographed rejoinder. Each of the four points was derided. The phrase "wherever practical," in (1), was designed, so it was said, simply to give the employers scope for misuse of agreements and as a sop to PLA representatives who were defending departmental work sharing schemes. The word "complete," in (2), was seen as a negative point, for an employer would only need to man part of his job with his own labor. As for (3) it would only negate the duties of shop stewards, and of (4) it was said that the trade unions would not demand withdrawal of employer licenses.

Although the discussions on continuity arrangements had some beneficial effect and helped move the strike toward settlement, the strike had not yet worked itself out and employers

[42] "Joint Statement," TGWU and NASD, Nov. 10, 1967.

still talked of letters of dismissal. It was suggested among them that one or two of their number who were in serious financial straights might send dismissal letters without the explosive effect if all employers did so. But there was real concern over continued division among themselves and some felt that even action by a few would only show that employers could not speak with one voice.

Replies which the employers received from their letter regarding modifications of continuity indicated that the terms of the new agreement were not fully understood. This suggested another letter on the subject — and was symptomatic of the problem of communication in the industry — but more important to the employers, perhaps, was their own need to reach agreement on a course of action toward men on strike and what might be done to relieve the cost of idleness created by their refusal to return to work. Some employers were more adamant than others about issuing dismissal notices as a first step to consideration of layoff of men. It was estimated that it was costing employers £ 70,000 to £ 100,000 per week.

It was not only the local employers who would be affected by a decision to take action. Employers and unionists elsewhere had a stake in the matter, even if it were not a financial one at the moment. The chairman of the London Port Employers Association said he would be obliged to advise the NAPE and the Minister of Labour before letters of dismissal could be issued. The PLA still did not feel in a position to send out dismissal notices to its employees on strike. It was still clear that the men would simply return to the Dock Labour Board with little likelihood that the Board could, or would, do anything. Hearing of the discussions and fearing the intention of sending letters of dismissal, the union leaders urgently requested a meeting, at which they raised strong objections, saying that such letters would seriously weaken their position and undermine their attempts to persuade the men to return to work and would almost certainly spread the strike.

At a meeting of both sides with the Minister of Labour in mid-November, the situation was reviewed in detail. Union leaders were critical of the publicity given to the activities of the unofficial element while little was given to the official ones. The Minister of Labour, however, was pleased that the employers were standing firm. On his part, he said he had no intention of dealing with the unofficial leaders.

Earlier, toward the end of October, it had been suggested among the employers in London that they should immediately grant the demand for the £ 17 guarantee. Some disagreed, saying that such action under the circumstances would boost the unofficial Liaison Committee and undermine the unions and weaken the authority of the leaders. But by mid-November the unions themselves lodged a claim nationally for an increase in the weekly guarantee to £ 16. Shortly thereafter, the Minister of Labour decided not to prevent implementation of the agreement that had been reached in London in March, to pay a weekly guarantee of £ 17. This paved the way for a settlement of the strike in London and the guarantee was raised elsewhere to £ 16 at a meeting of the NJC on December 28.

Modernization - Devlin Stage II

WITH the work stoppage settled and after a few months experience, a recapitulation showed less accomplished, as of the beginning of 1968, than had been originally intended or generally expected, at least as far as the employers were concerned, and especially among those in London. Most noteworthy, in view of the built-in promise, was the failure to achieve very much change in respect to flexibility and mobility. Due in part to apprehension about spreading or aggravating the stoppage — because they were not sure that the men would not react adversely or, conversely, because they feared that the leaders of the dissidents could arouse serious opposition — the employers in London had not taken full advantage of the clauses in the agreement dealing with flexibility and mobility. While a strong feeling developed among many of them in the early part of the year that the clauses should be effectuated in full as soon as possible, some wanted to proceed cautiously. Not all felt the same urgency, because their situations differed markedly. Those who wanted action felt that they should have their due in exchange for the major concessions made

to the unions and the men. The consensus among these was
that they should take full advantage of what was expected
and not be dissuaded by the unions simply because changes
might be unpalatable to some of the men. Others, whose interest in changing over to new methods or to mechanization
was not so immediate, wanted no disturbance of business
operations which they feared from opposition of enough men
to cause trouble in the port.

While it is difficult to pinpoint the matter, the employers,
taken as a group, knew that they themselves were not basically
sure of their own assessments. There was a hiatus between talk
and action. Yet, the initiative had to be theirs; they had to
make the move to modernization. The union leaders might
bless modernization but it was not their role to promote it.
Always, they had to be protective of the interests of the men —
aware of the differences among them — not to mention the
interests of the unions as institutions. The employers had to
decide whether or not they were prepared to meet the consequences of any moves toward modernization; really, whether
they could persevere in effectuation of their programs. Their
willingness to press vigorously was impeded by their knowledge that the union leaders, who expressed apprehension about
what would follow efforts at implementation of modernization,
were not usually able to control a large fraction of the men.
Could the employers weather opposition, even if from only a
minority of the men?

Two issues which had been foremost in negotiations in Stage
I and during the work stoppages, (1) payment to men when
idle due to a work stoppage — which had kept the agreement
negotiated by the NJC in the summer of 1967 a provisional
one — and (2) compulsory retirement, were "settled" insofar
as the unions were concerned; for the employers, neither was
settled satisfactorily. On the pay issue, the only recourse to
the employers, apparently, was to seek a new amendment to
the National Dock Labour Act, but the Minister of Labour
was not prepared to do anything — at least not until the Royal
Commission on Trade Union and Employers' Associations,

"the Donovan Commission," report was out. (It was not expected for some months and was not issued until the summer of 1968.) The unions would, of course, fight a new amendment of the National Dock Labour Act. As has been seen, the employers were not prepared to move, as a group, to discipline unofficial strikers; as will be seen, they would act tenderly on other matters of discipline, complaining that the law needed amendment in regard to this, too, in order to give them the role they needed, in spite of the fact that they had been assigned disciplinary power. On the issue of compulsory retirement the unions, with the men solidly behind them, had let it be known in no uncertain terms that no retirements would be compulsory.

Negotiating Problems Ahead

The negotiating problems ahead could not be separated easily one from another, because they were interrelated in various ways, but a number were easily identifiable and each of the parties realized that agreements had to be reached with respect to all. The mere listing does not reveal the importance, complexities, or interrelationships but does serve the useful purpose of identification. *Payment during strikes* and the problem of *mass indiscipline* have already been noted. The employers would keep the question of payment during strikes alive and would be concerned with other aspects of *discipline,* as well as mass indiscipline. Related to discipline was the agreement that a *shop steward system* would be developed, but there were problems about development and implementation. If compulsory retirement could not be revived by the employers, *retirement* was still an issue for both parties. Much attention was to be given to *voluntary retirement* and *severance pay.* Closely related to severance payments was the *size of the register* and tied to all the questions involving costs was the question of *wages,* both the system and the level. Other related matters, which represented costs to employers but benefits to workers, were *pensions, sickness payments,* and *holidays.* Benefits to employers, offsetting costs, were to be found in the solutions to the problems of *mobility and flexibility in assignment* of the men, and in *mechanization or modernization* agreements. With so formidable a list of problems, resolution was obviously not easy, and in London the situation was particularly mixed, complicated, and confused.

It was impossible to tackle all issues simultaneously. Day-to-day business had to go on, which produced its own needs and thrust some problems ahead of others. The differences within each side of the industry continued to be pervasive. More internal unity within and among the unions and among the employers would have simplified many matters, but, in the past, there was not enough unity among the parties on each side to produce a common facing. Within the ranks, agreement could not be reached even on relatively simple matters. For example, some employers in London wanted an understanding on overnight orders, so as to avoid delays in getting work started in the morning, but several with small labor forces preferred to have the men muster at a central point each morning for assignments. The employers could not agree on the issue. The basic difficulty was that they often lacked assertiveness – even when they did not lack unity of purpose – in carrying out their objectives. To be sure, they could not take full advantage of their due on mobility and flexibility – a cardinal point for them – without regard to the future of mechanization. For them, progress in mechanization was dependent upon adjustment of the number of registered men and the future control of the register, and both hinged on a future agreement on severance. That the unions and the men had their interests to defend or protect, the employers realized. Yet, it was more than disconcerting, after two successful modernization developments, Olsons at Millwall Docks and the OCL-ACT at Tilbury, to have London Docks Group No. 1 place a ban upon any further modernization agreements until an agreement for all could be reached. In January 1968, the following resolution was passed:

The Docks Group do not negotiate for any new methods of discharging or loading, or any mechanical operation which involves a reduction in the number of men employed as against conventional methods of operation until the whole of the Port of London is involved in a package deal.

The ban on new modernization agreements was not due to opposition to technological change. Improvements were wanted but equally for all. The men were jealous of the dockers who held the new jobs and feared that the "cream" of the work would gravitate to operations with new facilities, leaving men on conventional work with less desirable cargoes; ones on which they would have to work harder in order to make earnings satisfactory to them. Hence, they wanted to make sure that all men were to be treated equally; here, once again, the pervading philosophy of docker solidarity was manifesting itself.

Discipline

One of the aspects of modernization which presented problems, as listed above, was the matter of discipline. The industry had been stoutly criticized by the Devlin Committee for its lack of a shop steward system. This had not yet been realized and the administration of discipline by employers — long sought — was to become only a halting reality. The amendments in 1967 to the Dock Labour Scheme had given the employers the power to act in matters of discipline. Previously, it was the Board which acted following a complaint by an employer. Under the amended act, the Board became an appeals body only. Although they had long said they wanted the power, the employers, once they had it, hesitated to act. They even asked the unions for help but were told — and rightly so — that discipline was the employers' problem. Mostly, the employers did not want to precipitate confrontations. Nevertheless, moves were made to establish the shop steward system when the parties prepared sectional agreements setting out understandings on credentials, election procedures, representation, functions, discipline, facilities, duties, payments, and procedures for dealing with disputes.[43] Shortly, a shop steward problem arose. In the Royal Docks, it was contended that in all gangs having a shop steward a man, pro rata, should be employed to fill in while the shop steward was busy at steward's work. The employers rejected this proposal. As it turned out, it was not a strike issue because the workers were not convinced that special concessions should be made to shop stewards.

The problem of discipline continued to be troublesome, as the episodes involving the well-known militant in the Royal Docks, Jack Dash, illustrate. In December 1967, he was disciplined for convening an unofficial meeting during working hours. Workers claimed that action against a leader amounted to victimization, contending that all who participated should have been suspended. In a series of half-day strikes which followed, the employers took action against nearly three thousand men, giving two-day suspensions. Each man lodged an appeal. This so clogged the machinery that the Board requested the employers to withdraw their suspensions, which they did. It was demonstrated once again that the Scheme could not deal with mass indiscipline. But this is not the end of the matter.

In July 1968, Jack Dash and Buck Baker, the spokesman for the crane drivers, after being warned of possible suspension, nevertheless, went ahead and called unofficial meetings during working hours. Dash's meeting had to do with weekend work; and Baker's followed rejection by London PLEC of a claim for an increase in the allowance paid crane drivers. The two men were each given five-day suspensions without pay by Scruttons Maltby for holding unofficial meetings at the docks in working hours.[44] Dash won his appeal, although the four employers and four union representatives comprising the Board made it clear that they were not condoning unofficial meetings held during working time.[45]

---

[43]For example, "Shop Steward Procedure Within Member Companies (Stevedoring Section) of the London Ocean Traders Employers Association, Limited," mimeo., undated, but about January 1968.

[44]*The Port,* July 18, 1968, p. 1; August 1, 1968, p. 3.

[45]*Ibid.,* August 15, 1968, p. 16.

Scruttons Maltby gave Dash a five-day suspension a second time for holding a dock gate meeting in working hours on the subject of observing the Friday after Boxing Day as a holiday. The Dock Labour Board considered the matter and divided down the middle. There was no "casting vote," that is, a second vote by the chairman,[46] but the chairman, an employer, said he would not have used his second ballot even if he had one. Because of the division the suspension was "shelved."

Dash was again in trouble for two offenses in February 1969, when he was charged with breaking continuity for not reporting for work in spite of the fact that a leave of absence he had requested had been refused. This time the Dock Labour Board ruled that the suspension should be reduced from five days to one.[47] The disciplinary authority was obviously being applied with great caution.

Union Bargaining Demands

It is curious, particularly in light of the fact that the employers felt they had come out on the short end of Stage I, and in light of their own role as initiators of developments in modernization, that they allowed the Docks Group Secretary of the TGWU to take the initiative on February 28, 1968, to send a letter to the employers calling for an agreement. The TGWU wanted it to include, (1) a higher basic rate, (2) an increase in sick and accident pay and extension of period allowed, (3) an increase in pensions, (4) an increase in the holiday (vacation) period, and (5) a payment for voluntary severance. The TGWU said it would give "in return a free manning clause and a more modern service commensurate with new methods of work."

The London Modernization Committee thereafter met on March 22 and negotiations were resumed, but only in a desultory way because many difficulties beset employers. They felt they had to resolve the problem of severance before anything else.

---

[46]*Ibid.,* Jan. 2, 1969, p. 1.

[47]*Ibid.,* March 13, 1969, no. 50, p. 5.

Severance Payments

The NAPE had authorized local negotiations on severance payments after the Government had refused to make a contribution. The London Port Employers had held several meetings and were developing a severance payment scheme but could not divulge it at the time, because arrangements had not been completed for raising the necessary money. An added complication was the Government's announcement to nationalize the ports by January 1, 1970. The employers wanted assurance from the Government that in the event of nationalization they would be compensated for money paid out under a severance scheme. The unions did not want separate employer plans, but port-wide ones. In turn, of course, the employers emphasized that Devlin Stage II could not be disassociated from the size of the register; but the union spokesman pointed out that it was difficult to tell their members that negotiations with the employers could not go forward because of the dispute the employers were having with the Government about financing of severance payments. Yet, the union leaders agreed to join with the employers in again petitioning the Government for financial support, or assurances, regarding severance.

The union leaders were quite conscious of the continuing fear and uncertainty among dock workers as to the future. Enough employer closings or changes necessitating returning of men to the Dock Labour Board for reallocation kept the men disturbed, many clinging to the attitudes of the old casual system. It was apparent that fundamental change in attitudes on both sides was still to be achieved, modernization of thinking being a necessary condition of modernization of practices. The union leaders, however, in exchange for a satisfactory severance scheme and assurance of a satisfactory wage, seemed prepared to give a free manning clause, which the employers considered absolutely essential to real modernization. How to convince the doubters and obstructors among the men was the problem.

When no reply to their joint letter on financial support of severance payments had been received, although they were aware that it raised complex issues for the Government, the parties proposed a joint delegation to the Minister of Transport — particularly, because the Government had kept up the pressure for modernization. The employers wanted to continue negotiations on severance but felt it was quite wrong and misleading to the men to proceed without first having the assurance the employers requested of the Government; the union leaders, on the other hand, felt embarrassed to go back to the men and report no progress.

Another troublesome matter arose as certain wharfingers moved work outside the port area by establishing container depots, where the work of loading and unloading containers was performed by nonregistered men. The unions objected to handling containers coming from such depots and were prepared to take positive action to combat the development. Saying that they did not feel wharfingers could be prevented from opening inland depots, employers cautioned against industrial action. To make an industrial dispute of it, they said, would only serve to drive work away from the port to the disadvantage of all concerned. The union side, of course, found it illogical to be considering severance of registered workers while work which dockers could perform was being given to nonregistered workers away from the docks.[48]

Of other matters of deep concern to the parties, the most important was that no meeting of minds had been achieved on the structure of the wages system or on the level of wages. The TGWU, in a change of position, had voted to eliminate piece work and replace it with a higher basic rate of pay, an "upstanding wage," as it was called. The employers, while being willing to accept the elimination of piece work under new methods, still wanted some kind of incentive bonus and felt that piece rates should be retained on conventional jobs. Otherwise, so they

---

[48]This controversy ultimately led to the appointment of the so-called Bristow Committee which produced a statement concerning the extent of the port and a definition of dock work.

thought, efficiency would be impaired and the ships' stays would be prolonged.

On a related matter, employers wanted a two-shift system in order to make possible the greater utilization of modernized facilities once installed, but the ban on overtime had not been lifted and what chance was there of setting up two shifts if the overtime issue could not be resolved? The ban on overtime was as much a spread-the-work device as it was a device to avoid interruption of social life; the two-shift system promised to disrupt social life, for at least some of the men, as much as overtime.

Employers had problems of financing modernization. On the one hand, instituting modernization facilities would take funds and, on the other hand, money was needed to reduce manpower and to take care of severance payments. Where would the money come from? The general consensus was that each employer would have to pay for his redundancies, although a notion was current that a levy could be placed upon all shipowners and put into a central fund. Some contended that containers should pay a fair share, inasmuch as they would cause the redundancies.

In the spring of 1968, there seemed to be more discussion and bargaining about severance-pay schemes than anything else. This was a pressing problem to the employers if modernization ever was to be effectuated. As noted, an agreement on severance, including reduction of the register, was a necessary prelude to agreement on other matters. Many considerations and developments accentuated the difficulties of negotiating severance payments, such as removal of restrictive practices, rate of development of containerization, closure of docks, reallocation of men to different parts of the port — to Tilbury, for example — merger of employers, development of container consortia, and reorganization of shipping lines. The paradox was that once Devlin Stage II negotiations were completed, there would be a long sought flexibility and mobility which would cut manpower needs; this would necessitate control of the register and payment to men no longer needed. These dockers could not be compelled to leave the industry and had to be induced to do so. But how much severance payment and how finance it?

In May 1968, the unions reaffirmed, and made it clear indeed, that they were unalterably opposed to compulsory severance and contended that the voluntary severance scheme being proposed by the employers was not generous enough. They rejected compulsory severance even for the medically unfit, insisting that these men would voluntarily sever if given an adequate payment. If they did not, the union would reconsider compulsory severance for them at a later date. Employers, on their part, thought that if they had a national scheme, they might find it more feasible to gain reimbursement by the NDLB. Short of this, the general consensus was that the cost of redundancy should lie where it fell upon individual companies, except for the separation of the medically unfit who should be collectively covered. When no agreement was reached, the PLA prepared itself to go ahead with a voluntary scheme of its own. Some companies said, however, that the cost of their redundancy would be too great for the funds which they had to spare.

An interesting ripple was created, late in May, when employers took the position that voluntary severance schemes did not need to be negotiated. This caused the unions to consider it an outrageous affront contrary to established relations. It was doubtful whether schemes could be implemented without the approval of the work people's side. This the employers knew, and makes their suggesting a unilateral right the more mystifying. By late June the employers, anxious to establish severance schemes, presented the unions with certain adjustments in their proposal.

The PLA, in particular, was confronted with a special problem as a result of the closing of the London and St. Katherine Docks. It acted by sending letters to all the men, inviting them to apply for severance under the terms offered — original terms plus a terminal grant of £ 10 per man per year of service from 1942, the year satisfactory records were established

under the National Dock Labour Corporation. Also, consideration was given to permanent employees who had been employed
prior to 1942. The PLA agreed to a bonus payment of £ 40
to each retiree who could prove he had been registered in the
industry before 1942. Altogether, this made for a maximum
payment of £ 1,800. The unions expressed some disappointment
with the proposed bonus payment, yet, because the £ 1,800
was equivalent to £ 60 a year over thirty years of service, they
were prepared to recommend it to their constituents. As it
turned out, five hundred men accepted retirement voluntarily.

In July, with some agreement achieved on severance, most
employers were anxious to get on with negotiations under
Devlin Stage II, though there were differences in the ranks.
Some employers questioned whether the time had arrived for
such discussions, pointing out that they had not gained much
from Stage I — indeed, little more than a stable labor force —
and before negotiating further they should make sure in their
own minds that negotiations would be fruitful. Others felt
absence of Stage II agreements was creating new issues difficult
to resolve in the Ocean Trades. Meetings had to be convened
to achieve consensus. But they also had to keep meeting with
the unions.

The size of the register continued as a vexing problem. When
Hegarty, of the NASD, stated that the current labor force
was not large enough to meet requirements, the employers
said this was largely due to the lack of modern arrangements
for which the unions were partly responsible, because of the
ban on new modernization agreements. They constantly stressed
that mobility, mechanization, and reduced labor force were
necessary to make London competitive. In order to gain business in the port they said they had to modernize. Shea, of the
TGWU, reminded them of the points in his February letter,
and the promise that they would get free manning in exchange.
In turn, the employers reiterated their contention that progress
was being held up primarily because of the ban on new modernization agreements. They, of course, wanted the ban lifted
immediately.

The fact is that the top leaders in the unions were in a difficult position, the ban having probably been imposed in spite of them. Besides the concern of the men who were required to work conventionally and who had to put forth greater effort for less money than those working under modern terminal agreements — as well as suffering the discomfort of dirty jobs — there was the problem of the PLA taking over work hitherto performed by other employers and moving it to new locations. Feelings were running high among the men. They would not lift the ban until a package deal was negotiated providing equal treatment for all dock workers. Yet employers argued that the ban was costing work because, inasmuch as modern services could not be offered, it precluded obtaining new business. The men, they said, were defeating their own interests by refusing to contribute to modernization.

Nevertheless, the unions, expressing the views of the men, were adamant that work should be shared. A few should not be allowed to enjoy the better jobs while others had all the arduous tasks for lesser rewards. They remained unmoved by the argument that business was being lost as long as the employers were precluded from introducing new methods. Employers, in their turn, took the position that if reduced manning could not be realized, conventional manning and existing piecework rates would still apply, and kept requesting the unions to lift the ban on modernization agreements.

The ban on overtime was still annoying to the employers, with consequences similar to the ban on modernization agreements. They called upon the NASD to lift this ban, but the officials explained that a mass meeting had been convened at the request of certain branches and a decision against removal of the ban had been overwhelming. They said a further mass meeting could not be called until requested by the members; and the men, feeling that it would work against their interests, could not see the necessity to hasten the return to overtime working. Officials in the TGWU felt somewhat differently. They would support voluntary overtime; the individual should have the right to volunteer for overtime or to refuse. Hence, the problem, basically, was with the NASD.

The Statement of Intent

The demand of the unions to know the over-all policy of the employers led, in August, to an effort by the employers to draft a statement of intent, the unions having made it very clear that there was no possibility of the ban on modernization agreements being raised until such a statement was given and approved. But to produce such a statement required several months and, as will be seen, it was never really accepted although it went through various revisions.

In the fall, meanwhile, a "rift" appeared among the employers caused by the differing needs of employers in the Enclosed Docks and those on the Riverside. The London Wharfingers Association made the principles explicit upon which negotiations under Devlin Stage II could be carried out for the public wharfingers, noting that, in general, better conditions and earnings had been available to the men employed by the public wharfingers, who were primarily warehouse keepers, as compared with what the employers in the Enclosed Docks gave who were mainly concerned with the discharge and loading of ships. The Association also said it could not be bound by Stage II agreements reached between the employers in the Enclosed Docks and the unions, because the terms might not be acceptable to wharfingers. The wharfinger negotiations had to be entirely separate, and no Riverside employer would be required to adopt revisions of current working arrangements or wages structure under Stage II if such alterations would be economically impracticable for him.

In November, the employers in London offered their statement or letter of intent. In its preamble, they indicated their desire to achieve the objectives laid down by Lord Devlin for Stage II of modernization, but included the prerequisite that all existing bans on overtime and local productivity agreements be removed. Their main principles, basic to the anticipated productivity agreements, they then stated: the adjustment and maintenance of the size of the labor force for efficient and economic working of the port; complete mobility and flexibility in manning; operation of a two-shift system on the basis of a reduced working week; maintenance of an effective rate of working at all times; commitment to an agreed schedule of overtime and weekend working; acceptance of an effective disciplinary procedure; proper time keeping; and removal of all restrictive or protective practices. Apart from workers already employed under productivity agreements and those currently employed on a time-rate basis, the employers indicated they were studying the possibility of offering a productivity deal for those on piecework of £ 21 5s per week for a reduced basic working week set on the principle of shift work, with the provision of an equitable bonus. Sick and accident pay would be reviewed when details of the new national scheme were available. They were prepared to grant a three-week annual holiday under a program related to achievement of productivity. As for pensions, they were prepared to go beyond the forthcoming national negotiations, if necessary, but contingent upon transferability of funds and benefits from the national scheme. Sectional arrangements would have to be made in Lighterage, once the surplus labor problem was resolved, and some Riverside employers would need special consideration.

The unions thought the employers were a good deal more positive as to their requirements from the workers than they were explicit on what they were prepared to offer in exchange. Although willing to accept some of the enunciated principles, the TGWU wanted reference to shift work broadened to include other shift systems as might be agreed to sectionally. Also, the TGWU and the Lightermen were willing to accept the principles of voluntary overtime but on an agreed schedule to be negotiated. However, in the NASD, removal of the ban on overtime as a prerequisite to negotiations was not likely to be considered favorably. This union was standing on its earlier decision against any overtime. It also continued to oppose shift work. All the unions let it be known that ideally what they were interested in was a port scheme, although they were aware of special problems on the Riverside and in Lighterage. The unions accepted, in principle, the notion of a higher basic rate plus bonus but the amount offered by the employers as the basic rate they considered inadequate. They did not want sick and accident pay issues to await national agreement, nor did they want productivity "strings" tied to three-week holidays, but they were prepared to take one week in winter. Also, London should negotiate a pension supplementary to the national one. Shea explained that "free manning," promised in his letter in February, implied that manning was to be negotiated at sectional level according to the number of men needed for each job. But it was emphasized that it was only fair to the employers that they know the reluctance of many men to undertake any kind of shift working. On this point, employers thought that any initial reluctance might be overcome when the men studied the benefits to be derived from the employers' proposals. They emphasized that with some continental ports offering a 24-hour service on a 7-day week basis, they had to be prepared to meet the competition in quick turn around of ships.

The employers reminded the unions that it was implicit in the opening of negotiations on Devlin Stage II that restrictive practices would go, and they expected the unions and the men to yield. But union spokesmen cautioned that practices had been introduced by the unions for the protection of the men, and many were right and proper. Yet it might be possible, they conceded, to remove certain ones through negotiation. The unions told the employers they expected them to improve their letter of intent and urged a more liberal basic wage. They had already rejected £ 21 5s, plus a possible bonus of approximately £ 10. They seemed, then, to want something more like £ 26 or £ 27.

A national wage demand made at this time complicated negotiation of a modernization agreement. Employers held that the men could not expect increases under Devlin Stage II and national increases as well.

National Modernization Committee — Policy Statement

In December, the NMC issued a policy statement to all local modernization committees, designed to provide a basis for negotiations as well as a primer for action. It reaffirmed review of wages structure and abolition of all remaining restrictions to effective utilization of manpower and facilities, as envisaged in the Policy Directive of 1965 and stated as the substance of Devlin Stage II. It recognized that there would be a different pace within the respective ports, or even within ports, and that the process would be continuous. "Stage II," it said, "is not a once for all productivity deal." The objective was again stated: to modernize operations, improve economic performance, and to offer the best possible earnings opportunities to the men.

The NMC reaffirmed the need for nationally agreed-upon standards on time rates, weekly guarantee, holidays, sick leave, and pensions, but local improvements on these standards could be worked out with the consent of the NJC — for example, varying "the length of the working week...(when) coupled with...introduction of shift work." Ways to increase productivity were for the two sides to work out locally within the framework of the national policy. It was open to the two sides to work away from piece rates toward enhanced time-rate payments, supplemented by bonus payments related to productivity. Various suggestions or guidelines for achieving cooperation were made. Special attention was given to the need for a viable labor force, including review of registers and facilitating of natural wastage.

Removal or reduction of the piecework incentive would require work assessment and development of effective management, particularly at the supervisory level. The work of shop stewards would need development and attention. Hence, action at the local levels would necessitate deals on productivity, revision of pay structures, improvements over national minimum standards, flexible manning, shift working, elimination of any remaining time wasting practices, and voluntary severance arrangements. Difficulties not resolved locally would be referred to the NMC.[49]

---

[49]National Modernisation Committee, "Stage II Devlin, Policy statement to the local modernisation committees," Dec. 2, 1968, mimeo.

As the new year came on, other aspects of the total scene, in addition to the continuing controversy over the letter of intent, flashed before the parties. In January 1969, Barbara Castle, formerly the Minister of Transport and then the Minister of the Department of Employment and Productivity, issued a proposed policy for industrial relations, entitled *In Place of Strife*,[50] which was immediately buffeted by controversy and was bitterly opposed by unions throughout the country. Any glimmer of hope the employers in the docks industry had that it might be beneficial to them in ameliorating strikes on the docks was quickly snuffed out. It was proposed that the Minister be given a discretionary reserve power to secure a "conciliation pause," a euphemistic phrase for a "return to work," for a 28-day waiting period in unconstitutional (unauthorized) strikes and to have the discretionary power to hold a ballot on the question of strike action when an official stoppage threatened. Although the proposal was not adopted, it would have been interesting to witness its application to the docks to see if it could have had any effect on the actions of the dock workers.

Nationalization Announced

At the same time, the Government's plan on the reorganization of the ports was published.[51] The formal plans for nationalization of the docks were laid out with renewed notice that a bill to give legislative effect to the proposals was to be introduced in the 1969–1970 session of Parliament. While this gave a clearer picture of the Government's intentions, the state of politics in England at the time created uncertainty as to whether in fact any steps could be taken before a general election was held. Jack Jones, the new head of the TGWU and once a dock worker, made a forthright statement that nationalization was the only way out for the docks industry.[52]

---

[50]*In Place of Strife — A Policy for Industrial Relations* (London: Her Majesty's Stationery Office, Cmnd. 3888, January 1969).

[51]Ministry of Transport, *The Reorganization of the Ports* (London: Her Majesty's Stationery Office, Cmnd. 3903, January 1969).

[52]*The Port,* Jan. 30, 1969, p. 6.

It is of some interest that a proposal was made in January, also by Jack Jones, that the three dock unions in London merge. The proposal was given serious consideration, but the NASD was not very keen on it, and nothing came of it. In fact the NASD took the opportunity to reaffirm its ban on overtime.[53] It is interesting, by contrast, that a spokesman for the TGWU was prepared to say, "We will lift the ban [on new modernization agreements] when the employers put forward a satisfactory Letter of Intent that is acceptable for further talks."[54]

On with Negotiations

By February it was realized that the wrangle over the letter of intent had left the parties in a stage of impasse. The upshot was an understanding to set it aside — the employers claimed it was never intended as a negotiating paper — and to proceed locally along the lines of the policy statement of the NMC, concentrating on revision of the pay structure, improvement in minimum standards, flexible manning, shift working, elimination of time wasting practices, and voluntary severance arrangements. But differences plagued the employers. The Ocean Traders, expecting piecework to go and utilizing a greater number of men on ship work than the PLA, proposed a lower basic rate than the PLA and a higher bonus. They intended that the take-home pay would be the same as with the PLA workers, but the unions contrasted the £ 21, 5s basic rate offered by the Ocean Traders with the £ 29 put forward by the PLA and derided the former.

The employers, also, were having other trouble among themselves — mostly internal to their organizations but having an impact upon the men and the unions — about the rate of surcharge on transferred labor; mainly it was between the Ocean Traders and the Riverside employers. The charge on transfers of labor between employers was being negotiated among them. Until July 1968, the rate charged was 32 percent. Complaints led to a revision, effective from July 1, 1968, to the end of

[53]*Ibid.*, pp. 1, 8.
[54]*Ibid.*, Jan. 16, 1969, p. 3.

February 1969, which set the rate at 24 percent. The employer to whom men were assigned paid the cost of vacations, statutory holidays, sick and accident pay, national insurance, and bore certain administrative costs. These were calculated to be 15.25 percent of earned wages. But there was also the cost of wages paid if men were unemployed. This varied, employer by employer, because not every employer had the same experience. A figure of 15 days of unemployment along with the NDLB levy justified an additional 8.75 percent or the total of 24 percent surcharge. Therefore, to "borrow" labor, an employer had to pay the docker his wages plus a 24 percent payment to the loaning employer.

In March the tempo of negotiations between employers and unions so picked up that the No. 1 Docks Group Committee, which normally met quarterly, was meeting twice a week. At this time, the employers came forward with a new wage proposal, a three-tier structure, with differentials between time workers, men on the quay, and ship workers. Inclusive of bonuses, earnings would be £ 24, £ 32, 10s, and £ 34, respectively. There would be two shifts of 33¾ hours each week, weekend working on a voluntary basis, full flexibility and mobility, balanced labor force, and complete observance of the agreement by the men.[55]

The unions, in turn, soon issued a seven-page document, ostensibly some sort of answer to the points in the employers' letter of intent, in which they demanded £ 35 for a 35-hour week, two shifts a day, and voluntary weekend working.[56] But this is not to be interpreted to mean that the parties were in fact moving closer together; nor is the fact that at about this time the unofficial Liaison Committee disbanded in deference to the shop steward system.[57] More difficulties were ahead. Early in May the NASD held a mass meeting, in fashion typical of it, and by a good majority voted to reject any future pay and productivity agreement involving shift work. This

[55]*Ibid.*, March 13, 1969, p. 1, April 10, 1969, p. 2.

[56]*Ibid.*, March 27, 1969, p. 3.

[57]*Ibid.*, April 10, 1969, p. 16.

was countered in the TGWU by a decision of its three main groups, the Ocean Lay Committee, the PLA Committee, and the No. 1 Docks Group Committee, to go it alone and continue negotiations for an acceptable agreement, although they made it clear they did not want interunion war.[58]

In the early summer, matters appeared to be coming to some sort of head, conflicting viewpoints notwithstanding. Yet after two years of experience under Stage I, it was apparent that many shipowners, union leaders, and port workers were still not talking the same language, and that thinking needed to be modernized, as well as arrangements in the industry.

Viewpoints — Management and Labor

A comparison of some typical viewpoints expressed at this time are of interest.[59] Mr. John Kiernan, chairman, London Port Employers Association, an effective spokesman for employers, conceded that shipowners and employers had to change their attitudes drastically but that the unions and port workers had to do likewise. He felt the situation required urgent solution or London would face the consequences of remaining largely an unmodernized port to the detriment of all. He said "a golden opportunity must not be thrown away wantonly because of sheer stubbornness, conservatism, and short-sidedness." The Government must help in a courageous and nonpolitical way, but he did not want too much interference, which would be harmful. He, of course, like other employers was against nationalization. He wanted the unions to put their own houses in order, control their members, and be prepared to pay a price if they failed to deal with members who were in breach of agreements. He felt the unions had a duty to change their methods and wanted port workers to forget their old suspicions, give up outworn protective practices, and refrain from making continuous outrageous, uneconomic, and unreasonable demands.

[58]*Ibid.*, May 22, 1969, pp. 1, 2.

[59]*Ibid.*, July 17, 1969, pp. 3, 10.

Les Newman, leader of the NASD, said that his union could not get back to Stage II negotiations unless the terms of reference were altered. His members' instructions on shift work were rigid, however flexible on other working arrangements. He said the officers on the Enclosed Docks Modernization Committee had told the employers that provided they came forward with a document which did not have general shift working as a basis, then they were prepared to take it back to the membership and discuss it. He pointed out that they did not place a ban on all shift working, on particular ships or at certain berths, but they could not accept shift working as a general practice. Expressing the concern of his members, he said they wanted an industry in which there would still be jobs, not a ghost town of fast working machinery. He warned that in the event of their not being able to negotiate a Stage II agreement along the lines they proposed, and if the employers negotiated an agreement with anyone else, they would have to insist that Stage I proposals and levels of earnings, as far as his organization was concerned, would have to be adhered to.

On nationalization, Newman took issue with Mr. Kiernan, but said his union had not come to any set conclusion. They would be greatly interested in nationalization provided it took into account all ports, not leaving loopholes for other ports to expand at the expense of large ports like London and Liverpool. Nationalization would also be more acceptable to his union if it took in all container bases and warehouses, because they now found themselves in a position where employers were using various parliamentary acts to set up these bases to avoid use of dock labor. He also said that if nationalization in the sense that the Government had in mind meant acceptance of such things as *In Place of Strife,* they would have to be against it. He reaffirmed the long-standing practice of the union that at all times any new arrangement had to be approved by a mass meeting of his members.

Bill Lindley, of the Lightermen, said that nationalization was the key and that it had to be political, because one party would nationalize and the other would not.

Tom Cronin, a TGWU officer, accused the employers of delaying Stage II. He said "most employers in London are not conditioned to modern day thinking. Their attitude is that they cannot trust a dock worker to do a fair day's work if they pay a fair day's pay. Olsons have proved that this is not the case. If only London employers would agree right away to abolish piecework, they would eliminate one of the main causes of friction in this port." He accused the stevedoring firms of being the main retarders of progress — "They are not putting anything into the port but are delaying important negotiations." He had told the employers when they made their first wage offer, including a bonus incentive, that they were still thinking in the 1920's. The ban, he said, "had been brought about as a result of certain employers in port who are unwilling to adopt a progressive attitude," adding, however, that "there are some employers like the PLA and the shipping lines who are keen to make progress."

Cronin also said that if the ban were to be lifted, there had to be an unequivocal demonstration from the port employers that they were ready to improve their original offer for a new wage deal. The unions and the men felt that the existing offer of £ 24 as a basic guarantee, in the three-tiered proposal, was far too low for men who, through no fault of their own, had been forced into an unprivileged position. Many of the dockers in the light duty group were men who were casualties of a tough industry. Not all of them were near retirement age; many still had years of valuable contribution to make to the success of a modernized dock industry. It would be wrong, both in terms of social justice and good management, to condemn these men permanently to considerably lower pay packages because misfortune had hit them.

Governmental Conferences and Renewed Efforts

It was in the welter of these views but amid mounting pressures to come to agreement that, on July 10, a top level conference was held with the Minister in the Department of Employment and Productivity, attended by representatives of all the constituent groups in London, together with representatives from the NAPE. Of particular interest was the attendance of the entire No. 1 Docks Group Committee, because the ban on modernization agreements was a major point for discussion. Employers had increasingly expressed their impatience with the continuation of the ban. Afterward, it was felt by Government spokesmen that the meeting at the Ministry had achieved a real degree of communication, the pity being that it was not reached earlier. It was apparent that the leaders of the TGWU were mounting considerable pressure themselves for lifting of the ban, but they could not ignore the feelings of the men. Those in West India and Millwall Docks seemed to be for lifting the ban, whereas the men in the Royals generally favored retaining it. The men at Tilbury, in a mass meeting, voted overwhelmingly to retain it. It must be remembered, too, that the NASD had not taken part in any talks for a month, having withdrawn on the ground that they had no mandate from their members to discuss any agreement involving shift work.

Shortly after the meeting at the Ministry, the TGWU biennial conference convened, where consideration was given to a proposal the employers had made that October 1 be set as the target date for completion of Stage II negotiations, provided the ban were lifted immediately. As it turned out, the No. 1 Docks Group Committee, reading enough opposition among the men, overwhelmingly reaffirmed the ban on any further modernization agreements in London until all dockers were on a new agreement.

Another meeting was called by the Department of Employment and Productivity on July 28 to try to break the deadlock. The Government stated its grave concern over the situation, emphasizing the urgent need for settlement. The union leaders arrived first and stated their views on the ban; the employers stated that there was no way or justification for proceeding with negotiations until the ban was lifted.[60]

---

[60]*Ibid.*, July 31, 1969, pp. 1, 16.

In mid-August, although the deadlock still persisted, meetings were going on within the two sides to see if there was not some way around it. It would appear that the employers, in spite of their statements that negotiations could not go on so long as the ban existed, were keen to keep the talks going. They seemed resigned to the fact that the No. 1 Docks Group would not yield, accepting the argument, perhaps, that maintenance of the ban was the only way the TGWU could keep control of the situation in London. If the ban were lifted, particularly in light of the strong expressions from the Royals and Tilbury to maintain it, the way would be opened for the reemergence of the unofficial Liaison Committee. This was to be avoided at all costs. Even then, its influence was still felt. In resumption at the end of August of unofficial half-day strikes in the Royals, called by the shop stewards, it was obvious that individuals, previously active in the unofficial Liaison Committee, were then active as shop stewards.

While it had its ludicrous side, the Tilbury leaders agreed to conventional manning at the OCL Berth at Tilbury. This new facility had been standing unused because of the ban. The interest on the investment was calculated to cost half a million pounds a year. Conventional manning would make possible its use on this limited basis until the ban was lifted. The Tilbury dockers, however, rejected the plan at first. It is of interest that TGWU leaders and the Enclosed Docks employers, about this time, reached an agreement on hours and shift work, setting shifts to run from 7:00 A.M. to 2:00 P.M. and 2:00 P.M. to 9:00 P.M., totaling a working week of 31¼ hours. The agreement, of course, had to be confirmed by the men. Overshadowing it was the insistence of the NASD that it wanted no part of any agreement that included shift work.

Two major hurdles, in addition, remained: (1) sanctions sought by the employers regarding discipline and (2) pay. The employers' three-tier structure was not opposed outright, yet the union was having difficulty accepting the rate of £ 24 for time- or light-duty workers who, according to the view of the union, were being victimized through no fault of their own by virtue of their employment status. Meetings went on in September, with the TGWU increasing its demand to £ 37, 10s a week, plus a 5 percent bonus for all ship and quay workers, and £ 28 for light-duty men, at the same time letting it be known that it would not agree to individual employers having the power to hire and fire. But the NASD kept reiterating that, whatever was agreed to, it was not taking part in the talks.

Enclosed Docks Agreement — First Vote

Later in the autumn the employers, staying with the three-tier wage structure, made a "final" proposal for the Enclosed Docks, offering light-duty men £ 24 a week, quay workers £ 32, 10s, ship workers £ 34, and a 5 percent bonus for quay and ship workers. This was based on the previously agreed $31\frac{1}{4}$ hour week.[61] The Riverside employers were standing on an offer of about £ 24, for a normal day's work. Not, generally, contemplating shift work, they were intending to continue on a piece-rate system.[62]

Negotiations for the Enclosed Docks produced a sufficient meeting of minds to warrant submitting the matter to the men. For the first time in the history of the docks, the employers' offer was put to the men by mail ballot. Heretofore, voting had always been in the lay committees or in mass meetings by voice vote. Because the proposal covered only the Enclosed Docks, the men in this area were the only ones polled. Each docker was given a copy of the full proposals and a week to consider them. Mass meetings were held in various sections during working hours, where union officials addressed the men and answered questions. The officials, however, did not endorse the proposal or urge acceptance, leaving the men completely free to make up their minds independently.[63] It was understood, of course, that agreements for the Riverside, Clerks, and Lightermen would have to be made before they could

[61]*Ibid.*, Sept. 11, 1969, pp. 1, 16.

[62]*Ibid.*, Oct. 23, 1969, p. 1.

[63]*Ibid.*, Nov. 6, 1969, pp. 1, 16.

implement this agreement. And the NASD was a group to be contended with, having again restated its objection to shift work.

To get one of the 8,500 printed ballots a man had to be paid up; 7,101 ballots were claimed. Almost 80 percent who took ballots voted. The dockers voted, "No," by a count of 3,090 to 2,442, with 1,558 ballots not returned. Some who were enjoying earnings of £ 40 a week felt they would lose income while having to work shifts. Others were against shift work outright, whether due to disruption of social life or fear that it would cost jobs. Many thought the wage offer too low. Some perhaps were just against change or felt the employers were gaining more than they were giving.

On the other hand, there were those who were troubled because of the negative vote and the failure of a good proportion of the men to cast ballots. Some were afraid, owing to the failure to get on with modernization, that they would lose work as the port lost business. One said, "The men must be mad to turn down an offer like that." There should have been more leadership from the union, some felt, and said that the decision of union officials not to recommend acceptance of the proposal was unfortunate and contributed to the outcome.[64]

National Modernization Chairman

Early in 1970, talks had to be resumed — and were — in spite of the employers' previous "final" offer. But there were other developments. Mr. George Cattell, the independent chairman of the National Modernization Committee, speaking in mid-January at Thurrock Technical College, Tilbury, used the occasion to express his views frankly about the situation in the docks industry. If his remarks were somewhat controversial and not relished in some quarters, nevertheless, his was a considered judgment of the situation at the time and is worthy of note, in view of his position and also because it is a cogent review which brings events into focus. He criticized both man-

---

[64]*Ibid.*, Dec. 4, 1969, pp. 8, 9.

agement and union leaders for lacking foresight in planning
and for lack of responsibility in shouldering the obligations
Devlin thought they should have carried. He was not unaware
of "the problem of overcoming the efforts of generations of
casual and uncertain employment and of payment only for
tons or pieces lifted," but he thought the shipowners short-
sighted in not foreseeing "the predictable changes in cargo-
handling methods and the equally predictable social changes
which were to expose the casual system of employment as a
stupid and uneconomic practice."

It had taken, Cattell noted, fifty years of "hardship and bitter
struggle for the docker to achieve the privilege of a reserved
but still casual occupation [the guarantees under the National
Dock Labour Scheme]. Small wonder that he now sometimes
appears suspicious and obstinate." He charged the shipping
companies with "an aloof detachment from the problems of
port operation," while often exerting "pressure on the unfortunate stevedoring employers to concede quite unjustifiable
and inflationary wage demands if and when backed by the
threat of unconstitutional strike action." (The same charge
is valid in other ports, for example, the Port of New York.)
Nevertheless, he was willing to state that in the five-year period
from 1965 to 1970, "far more has been accomplished in terms
of employment and of productivity than in the previous fifty."
For the country as a whole, the 58,300 dockers in 1965 had been
reduced to 46,600, whereas tonnage had increased from 100
million to 104 million tons; that is, 12,000 fewer men handled
4 million tons more. But, he had to add, "the promise of
Devlin has so far not been fulfilled," whereas, if "employers
and union officials had. . .matched the enthusiasm with which
they greeted the Devlin Report, we should now be in a much
more advanced stage than we are."

Noting that the 1966 pay settlement was a sort of "payment
on account" for the abolition of "what were called restrictive"
but "better termed protective" practices, and "the launching
pad for the steady upward lift in earnings and benefits enjoyed by registered dockers" who were now "on permanent

employment...and on terms probably more favourable than those enjoyed by workers in any other industry," Cattell said, it was expected that the workers would "soften their militancy" but "it was not to be." The employers were disappointed. He thought it a discredit to the union leaders that "having secured a favourable interim wage settlement and having subscribed to a far-reaching national policy directive, then they more or less sat back and allowed the law of the jungle to prevail." He was far from meaning that nothing had been accomplished, for, in addition to enactment of the Docks and Harbours Act of 1966, the initiation of the scheme of licensing of employers, and the amendment of the Dock Labour Scheme, under which allocation of the men had been achieved, he listed the other accomplishments to the end of 1967: "In the space of about two years the industry had abolished the casual system...introduced a basic weekly wage plus a special modernization payment, abolished attendance money, introduced a guaranteed minimum weekly wage...improved its pension benefits, introduced a sick pay scheme...eliminated a number of time-wasting practices and substantially reduced the numbers of licensed employers and registered dockers."

Comparable measures, Cattell admitted, had taken more than two decades in most other industries, but more could have been accomplished. Since the national policy statement adopted in December 1968, a statement which had taken three months to negotiate and draft, leaving the ports at the beginning of 1969 in a position to negotiate the remaining goals of Devlin, he noted that little progress was made. To be sure, there was no single objective "like nationwide decasualization," for change had to be "a continuous process," but negotiations in the major ports, notably London, had bogged down. Voluntary severance had been a major hurdle and the Government unwisely refused to help the industry reduce its manpower; only belatedly did it come forward with "the necessary initial funds." He saw the manpower problems at the heart of the stalemate, partly because the industry had not planned ahead sufficiently and had not carefully estimated its future needs under the burgeoning new technology. To him, solution of the manpower problem could not await the launching of a new National Ports Authority.

The main reason why Devlin Stage II had not produced more, Cattell continued, was due to the hiatus in authority and control between the national and local levels with "actions of both the registered dockers and the licensed employers... sometimes...in total disregard of the principles subscribed to by their representatives in the National Modernization Committee." Manning problems, he felt, had to be worked out jointly but he found no need, under guaranteed employment, to continue the existence of the Dock Labour Boards, certainly not under the projected nationalization. He said, "I cannot understand the desire to preserve the Dock Labour Scheme, which the dockers really deserved, but I suspect that it is now leading us into an impenetrable and totally unexplored jungle. Registration and the Dock Labour Scheme were, and still are, protective practices for an old and much bruised industry." The old traditional ways, he felt, were rapidly going and would disappear under the impact of the new technology. His prediction: the docker of the future will be a highly paid specialist with the dignity and rewards of a highly paid specialist; his final appeal, "cut our losses and forget the past conflicts."[65]

Jack Jones' Rebuttal

A sequel to Cattell's prepared speech, a strong rebuttal, came from Jack Jones, who a month or so later also spoke at Thurrock Technical College. He declared that the unions and the men would rule out completely any move to phase out the Dock Labour Scheme. The union was willing to talk of changes "provided the principle of joint control of labour was retained....We regard the registration scheme like indentures for trained apprentices. It [strangely] represents a property right which we will strongly defend." He took the opportunity to reiterate the union's position on this matter as it related

---

[65]G. H. B. Cattell, "Devlin Stage II — A Tragedy in the Modern Style." Talk delivered at Thurrock Technical College, Jan. 13, 1970, mimeo.

to the question of nationalization. Being critical of the "watered down" program of nationalization in the pending bill, he emphasized the demand for one employer; but because the bill was not all-inclusive he asserted that continuation of the Dock Labour Scheme without change was imperative. He called attention to the barrage of statements about big cuts being made in port labor and the fears this created in the men, adding, "This is certainly not the time to talk of reducing the degree of joint control which at present plays such an essential part in the registration scheme." Instead, he emphasized, it was time to talk of progressive changes which would extend the principle and practice of joint control. He wanted various joint committees of equal numbers of management and union representatives, stressing the need for members of Port Authorities experienced in organization of workers within the industry. He wanted created a "real partnership between management and workers on a real basis of joint control." (It must be kept in mind that under his version of nationalization, management would be a governmental body, including equal representation from the docks industry.) If the parties did not want to lose large sums of money on disputes, they should be prepared to spend a relatively small sum on participation.

Jones said, "There are thousands of men in our industry who already have knowledge and the ideas which management seems quite willing to pay thousands of pounds to consultants to provide quite inadequately." Why not tap the knowledge of the men who were competent because of their experience. Bluntly, he was looking for a transfer of some decision-making. Wages were not enough, he insisted; what was needed was involvement and participation of the men. "The crisis feeling here in London cannot be underestimated. The closures of docks and wharves which have already taken place, together with projected changes, all contribute to a state of frustration and concern by many employed in the port." He warned, "the massive investment in the industry is to little purpose without a cooperative staff and labour force." He thought "pillorying the dock workers as old-fashioned and obstructive" had to stop because average tonnage handled per man had increased 25 percent since decasualization. And his version of the ban at Tilbury was not just about containers but was integral to the whole problem of modernization.[66]

Fruitful Negotiations

Crucial meetings of the Enclosed Docks employers and the leaders of the TGWU had convened, beginning with one on January 23. The employers agreed to come up with a new pay offer, but the price of Stage II seemed to go up again. Fifteen months earlier, the employers had offered £ 21, 5s a week plus a 50 percent bonus, which would have produced, for most men, total weekly pay of £ 31, 17s, 6d. Shortly thereafter, the TGWU had asked for £ 35 for all men. Two months later, the employers offered £ 32, 10s to quay workers and £ 34 a week to ship workers and said they wanted to do away with all forms of incentive bonuses. The union then stepped up its claim, first, to £ 36 and, then, to £ 37, 10s a week. In retrospect, it was felt that had the employers accepted the union's earlier demand for £ 35, a settlement on Stage II would have followed quickly. Now, the union renewed its claim for £ 37, 10s, adding a 5 percent bonus designed to produce a basic wage of £ 39, 7s. Olsons was paying £ 39 for a thirty-hour week, and the unions kept an eye on this. In fifteen months, the wage demand had increased by approximately £ 10 a week.[67]

Early in February, the Enclosed Docks employers made their new offer, based on a weekly wage of £ 29, 10d, plus incentive bonuses. "The employers," said one, "felt they could not pay extra money unless it was allied to an incentive system." They had set standard target figures for different commodities to be reached before the men would qualify for bonuses. The parties seemed to reverse positions on the matter of incentives. As of this time, the union had decided against continuation of piece rates. The employers made it clear that they had not withdrawn

---

[66]*The Port*, Feb. 26, 1970, p. 15; March 12, 1970, p. 7.

[67]*Ibid.*, Jan. 29, 1970, p. 1.

their previous offer of an "upstanding wage" with no bonus, should the union want to reconsider it.[68]

The Government's Ports Bill

Meanwhile, the Government's Ports Bill providing for nationalization of the docks was being debated in the House of Commons.[69] Designed to implement the White Paper, *The Reorganization of the Ports,* issued in 1967, the bill, nevertheless, departed in certain respects from some of the recommendations made by the Government at the earlier time. Whereas it had been projected that the functions of the NDLB would be integrated into the new national ports authority, the bill remained silent on this matter — no doubt a concession to the unions. Also, the bill exempted ports handling less than 5 million tons of cargo a year, and it placed in the hands of the ports authorities the decision as to the facilities to be taken over within a port and the timing of such take over. The vesting day, of course, had not been set and would emerge only later; furthermore, no facilities could be taken over short of twelve months after such a date. These things, in particular — many aspects of the bill being highly controversial in the political context of Great Britain — created a good deal of uncertainty and controversy. When, if at all, would the bill be accepted? Would it be passed by the time the Prime Minister called for an election? If the Labour Party lost, what then?

The left-wing adherents in the Dock Workers Section of the TGWU, supported by the new general secretary of the TGWU, Mr. Jack Jones, were critical of the bill. They pursued a program of inclusion of 100 percent of the ports, 100 percent of the facilities, and 50 percent of the control. The latter demand, of course, was more than had been written into any bill of nationalization, but it squared with the viewpoint, advocated by Jones and the Institute for Workers Control and supported by prominent left-wing personalities in the unions, industry,

[68]*Ibid.,* Feb. 12, 1970, p. 1.
[69]*Ports Bill,* Bill 48, printed Nov. 26, 1969.

and the academic field, that what was needed was more "factory floor" participation.[70]

Enclosed Docks Agreement — Second Vote

On February 24, an agreement for the Enclosed Docks was accepted by the negotiators and was again set for consideration by the men under a mail ballot. It provided for two categories of men, category A being men fit to undertake actual cargo-handling operations and category B those not physically fit for strenuous work. The definition of categories was explicitly stated. For category B, the weekly pay was set at £ 26. For category A, the weekly wage was set at £ 34, 10s, with a 10s differential per shift while working as a part of a ship's gang, making a weekly wage of £ 37 for those workers. No bonus was offered; the wage incorporated the modernization allowance from Stage I and was based on the understanding that all additional time payments included in the old structure were discontinued. Any additional income would have to come from working overtime, which was to be voluntary. Shift work, of course, as previously agreed to was included. Explicit "time-keeping" rules were laid down to assure control over both attendance and promptness. Both categories of men were given identical annual holidays at a standard payment of £ 32, 10s per week, with the men taking one of the three weeks during winter. Rules were spelled out governing manning, flexibility, and mobility; temporary transfer policy; turning out money; and fares. A statement on observance of the conditions of the agreement was included and procedures for settlement of grievances were set out in detail, with slight variation in the steps between the Ocean Trades and the PLA.[71]

Ballots had to be returned by March 18, to be counted on March 20. It seemed quite clear that this was the very last

---

[70]Institute for Workers' Control, *The Dockers Next Steps;* cf. Parliamentary Debates, House of Commons, Official Report, Standing Committee D, *Ports Bill*, Twentieth Sitting, March 17, 1970, Part I, pp. 1180, 1184.

[71]"Enclosed Docks Productivity Agreement (Dockworkers other than Ships Clerks)," Feb. 24, 1970, mimeo.; *The Port*, Feb. 26, 1970, pp. 1, 5.

offer the employers could make. A note of optimism pervaded the ranks on both sides, however. Again, the men had to pick up their ballots and 6,442 were issued, considered to be 90 percent of the men eligible. The new offer was debated widely. This time, the union officials and lay committees recommended acceptance and, again, meetings were held throughout the port.[72] What was disconcerting to some, however, was the stand taken by the NASD and the fact that it issued a leaflet throughout the Enclosed Docks saying, "Had we still been involved in Phase II negotiations we would have recommended our members to reject the proposals."[73] They, of course, were opposed to shift work and still maintained a ban against overtime work. Also, they thought the wages should be something on the order of £ 39 or £ 40 a week.

Parliamentary Debate over Nationalization

As the meetings over the new offer and preparations for the balloting were taking place, the debate in Parliament over the Nationalization Bill was going on in the House of Commons. The left-wing of the dockers union, as already noted, did not like the Government's version of the bill. Even if the National Dock Labour Board was left intact, the bill excluded certain small ports and gave the port authorities the power to decide what facilities would be taken over and when. It also followed the pattern set in other bills on nationalization which, in providing for labor representation in management, nevertheless, provided that it come from the ranks of labor outside of the industry. The ardent nationalizers in the dockers union and the left-wing of the Labour Party felt the Government had emasculated the proposition of nationalization and they wanted it rectified.

It is a curious coincidence, perhaps, that on the day set for return of the ballots on the Enclosed Docks Agreement, an "unofficial" strike and mass meeting at Tower Hill took place, followed by a march to Westminster for a further demonstra-

[72]*The Port*, March 12, 1970, pp. 1, 8, 9.

[73]*Ibid.*, p. 8.

tion against the bill.[74] The essence of the unionists' position, at least of the more ardent left-wingers, was that they wanted more nationalization and more worker control. The cry was "100 percent of the ports, 100 percent of the facilities, and 50 percent of the control," as mentioned above.

In March, the Government had announced its selection of Peter Parker as the first chairman of the projected National Ports Authority. He was a professional manager and was chosen for his knowledge of "the business of business," not because of expertness in the docks industry. His appointment to some in the unions could not be disassociated from their dislike of the bill, "the watered down version of workers' participation," as it was described. Nor did they like the names of the six named members. Regarding Parker's first statement, when his job was announced — "What those of us who are professional managers have to do is make sure the entrepreneurial kick is given scope in national business" — it was said: "In plain man's language that means he wants to kick the dockers into redundancies and into making big profits to subsidize the shipowners and other business interests who use our ports." They wanted, instead, "extension of nationalisation to all ports and harbours, and all private employers of port labour, simultaneously;" "extension of worker's representation in the management of the port industry;" and "extension of the powers of joint control exercised under the National Dock Labour scheme." They were angry and felt betrayed by the Government they helped into office.[75] The aroused dockers were prepared to take vigorous action, but, as reflected in the meagre crowd which assembled at Tower Hill, the mass of dockers were probably not too concerned. In fact, many of the dockers were for nationalization primarily because they equated it with preventing redundancy in the industry, a matter which promise after promise from employers and Government could not seem to resolve.

By tolerating in the corridors of Westminster the dockers

[74]Parliamentary Debates, House of Commons, op. cit., Parts I, II, III.
[75]The Port, March 12, 1970, p. 4.

who were on an unofficial strike, which was not about wages or working conditions but to achieve amendments to a bill — a strike of dubious legality, an industrial action for political ends — the Minister was accused by Conservative spokesmen of being intimidated. The Minister's effort to hold all-night sessions in order to get on with the debate was considered a "remarkable coincidence" with "the appearance of dockers," and the Conservatives complained that they were "sitting under duress."

The debate concerned the pros and cons of nationalization of the docks, but the efforts of the left-wing to introduce amendments in order to achieve greater, and direct, worker participation in management — not just policy formulation — aroused deep feelings. The Conservatives became real defenders of collective bargaining and argued that the type of worker control proposed in amendments from the left was "a serious threat to industry, to our trade unions and to our whole system of collective bargaining...the first step on a slippery slope which would lead to industrial anarchy." But the rationalization for more worker participation than had been provided in any other bill on nationalization was expressed by Mikardo, "I do not believe that anybody can represent a group of people unless he is chosen by those people, answerable to them and recallable by them."[76] The Government's version of the bill withstood onslaughts both from the left and from the Conservatives, passed in the House of Commons, and went on to the House of Lords.

For the record, a minor anomaly must be briefly noted. Even though Jack Dash and his followers in the unofficial Liaison Committee had almost always opposed what the leaders of the Dockers Section of the TGWU proposed, and for years had been notorious as disruptors of the Port of London, once Dash was eligible for retirement with severance pay, he accepted severance with alacrity and bowed out of the industry.[77]

[76]Parliamentary Debates, House of Commons, *op. cit.*, pp. 1112–1113, 1124, 1188 ff.

[77]*The Port,* Feb. 26, 1970, p. 5.

Implementation of Agreements

With the balloting on the Enclosed Docks agreement over, on March 20, the vote was counted: 4,137 voted to accept, 1,880 voted to reject, and 17 ballots were spoiled. As a result 70 percent were for acceptance.[78] Nearly everyone was happy with this outcome but much was still ahead. The controversy over nationalization, as noted, was still running. Other agreements, with other groups, the Clerks, the Riverside, and the Lightermen, not to mention the ancillary employees, had to be worked out. And there was the perennial question of the NASD. Even so, a staging day was set for June 29, 1970. The Riverside agreement was quickly worked out and accepted. To the gratification of almost all, the ban on further modernization agreements was soon lifted.[79] There had been good reason to expect that it would be lifted because a number of men who were on the negotiating team for the union were also members of the No. 1 Docks Group Committee. The real question ahead turned on the NASD. Could this union be induced to retreat from its position or would it be possible to move on in spite of it?

The National Election — Dropping Nationalization

Suddenly on this scene fell Prime Minister Wilson's call for a national election. This had the effect, under British constitutional law, of washing out all pending legislation, notably the Nationalization Bill. At first this only presented the prospect of reintroduction of the bill, or a new one, for it was generally expected that the Labour Party would win. But the surprising victory of the Conservative Party wiped out the question of nationalization as a legislative possibility. The Conservatives had promised only a strengthened Ports Authority.

The National Strike over Wages

While the calendar moved inexorably on toward June 29, the parties in London were overtaken by another development. A national wage demand had been made as far back as De-

---

[78]*Ibid.*, March 26, 1970, p. 1.

[79]*The Times* (London), April 2, 1970, p. 17; April 24, 1970, p. 1.

cember 1967 and had been kept alive by periodic renewals. At this juncture it came rapidly to the fore. Whether the victory of the Conservative Party had anything to do with the pressure on the national wages claim is not clear, but some thought the political change gave impetus to the push to resolve it. In any case, implementation of the Enclosed Docks agreement was not undertaken on June 29, largely because the NASD had not retreated from its position and the employers feared that this union could precipitate a walkout. It is not likely that the deadline set on national bargaining had much to do with it; in fact, the Riverside agreement was implemented in early July, the NASD not being involved. Meanwhile, the Docks Group No. 1 threatened the employers, contending that they were required to implement the Devlin Stage II agreement for the Enclosed Docks. But the TGWU had set a deadline for a strike on July 15 if an agreement on the national wage claim was not reached. Feverish bargaining on it, including sessions with officials of the new Government, failed to produce an agreement and the first national dock strike since 1926 was called.

The strike ran on until August 3, involving the British public and the economy, not to mention the new Government, in a trying experience. Settlement came only after Lord Pearson, who had been appointed chairman of a Court of Inquiry, worked out a compromise acceptable to the parties.

The Pearson Court of Inquiry recognized that the national wage claim was really a matter of much less importance than the negotiations on Devlin Stage II:

The port transport industry is in the course of making a major, far-reaching and vitally important transition from the old fashioned and relatively inefficient methods of working and an archaic, complex and not wholly rational pay structure to new and much more productive methods of working and a simplified and rational pay structure.

It added that these negotiations had to be actively pursued and nothing done to hinder them. It found that the issues in the national controversy had a "temporary character" and

would "largely disappear" when Devlin Stage II agreements
went into effect. Compared to the latter, the national wage
claim was an anomaly, genuine enough with respect to certain
matters, but interim relief could be granted.[80]

Contrary to widespread and distorted publicity in the United
States that the British dock workers were demanding increases
in pay of 80 percent,[81] the Court found that the national wage
claim "was not intended to produce any general increase in
the earnings of dock workers." It was a matter of general consequence for only about 16 percent of the dock workers in small
ports where Devlin Stage II negotiations were inappropriate.
Otherwise, the claim was designed only to raise the minimum
time rate in relation to stand-by, overtime, and holiday payments. It was not intended to apply to piece rates. Furthermore, the Court of Inquiry found that the average earnings of
dock workers — this, before the modernization agreements — ex-
ceeded £ 35 per week and that dock workers were not under-
paid compared with other workers for all industries, where
average earnings were under £ 25 per week. The minimum
time rate was outmoded but, since it had application primarily
only to calculation of stand-by, overtime, and holiday payments,
it was not difficult to work out a settlement. The employers
offered to increase the fall-back guarantee from £ 16 (£ 17 in
London) to £ 20 per week. The Court held that the guarantee
should be on a daily basis, that is, £ 4 for eight hours without
overtime. It also made recommendations for the calculation
of overtime and holiday pay. They were accepted by both
parties.[82]

"Final" Settlement

With the national wage dispute settled, and without preju-
dicing Devlin Stage II settlements and negotiations, the em-

---

[80]*Report of a Court of Inquiry under the Rt. Hon. the Lord Pearson,
C.B.E. into a dispute between the parties represented on the National
Joint Council for the Port Transport Industry* (London: Her Majesty's
Stationery Office, Cmnd. 4429, July 1970), p. 15 ff.

[81]*New York Times,* July 13, 1970, p. 50; July 17, 1970, p. 1.

[82]*Ibid.,* July 28, 1970, p. 2; July 30, 1970, p. 1.

ployers and the unions in London moved on toward further
settlements and, finally, to implementation. As noted, the Riverside agreement was implemented early in July. The Enclosed
Docks agreement, with the NASD joining in its signing — despite the history of emphatic protestations against it — was
implemented on September 21.[83] The Lighterage agreement
had not then been completed, owing mainly to the large surplus of men and the difficulties of fitting in both with the
shift system in the Enclosed Docks and with the 8:00 A.M. to
5:00 P.M. workday on the Riverside; there was also a problem
with the foremen. But the major hurdles had been cleared and
a new day dawned — almost three years to the day and after
three years of anguished negotiations — with general satisfaction across the board. The historic date of decasualization,
September 18, 1967, was now matched with the date of modernization, September 21, 1970, and the way was cleared for
movement to a new era on the docks. Democratic, private
decision-making, albeit with some governmental assistance —
British style — had come through with an interesting chapter
in the history of collective bargaining. Problems will still be
faced, but the future should be substantially different from
the past. Dock workers will enjoy better working conditions,
better pay on a regular basis — a dream some had had more
than a half century — and the industry will be in better condition than ever before to make itself efficient and competitive
in the midst of the revolutionary changes taking place in the
industry. Nationalization may still come one day but British
politics will decide this issue. Meanwhile, the docks industry
has achieved a noteworthy accomplishment, and the men and
their leaders and the employers and their associations can look
with satisfaction upon the results of their long labors. Democratic decision-making has added another solid accomplishment.

[83]*Productivity Agreement (Devlin Stage II) concluded by the Enclosed
Docks Employers (LOTEA and PLA) with TGWU and the NASD,* Sept.
15, 1970.